NORTH MACEDONIA

TRAVEL GUIDE

2023

A Journey of Majestic Landscapes, Ancient Wonders, and Exquisite Delights

ZARA EXPLORES

COPYRIGHT©2023 ZARA EXPLORES

ALL RIGHTS RESERVED

TABLE OF CONTENTS

INTRODUCTION TO NORTH MACEDONIA 6

CHAPTER 1 10
    COUNTRY OVERVIEW 10
    GEOGRAPHY AND CLIMATE 12
    CULTURAL BACKGROUND 14

CHAPTER 2 18
    ESSENTIAL TRAVEL INFORMATION 18
        Entry Requirements and Visa 18
        Currency and Money Matters 24
        Language and Communication 26
        Transportation within Macedonia 28
        Safety and Security Tips 31

CHAPTER 3 34
    PLANNING YOUR TRIP 34
        Best Time to Visit 34
        Duration of Stay 36
        Choosing Your Destinations 38
        Budgeting and Expenses 40
        Packing Essentials 42

CHAPTER 4 46
    EXPLORING SKOPJE 46
        Skopje City Overview 46
        Must-Visit Attractions 48
        Cultural and Historical Sites 50
        Shopping and Dining Recommendations 52
        Nightlife and Entertainment 55

CHAPTER 5 58
    DISCOVERING OHRID 58

- Ohrid City Overview ... 58
- Ohrid Lake and Natural Beauty ... 60
- UNESCO World Heritage Sites ... 62
- Water Activities and Beaches ... 64
- Local Cuisine and Traditional Crafts ... 66

CHAPTER 6 ... 70
Venturing into Other Regions ... 70
- Matka Canyon ... 70
- Mavrovo National Park ... 72
- Bitola and Pelister National Park ... 74
- Kratovo and Kuklica Stone Dolls ... 76
- Stobi Archaeological Site ... 78

CHAPTER 7 ... 82
Cultural Experiences ... 82
- Macedonian Festivals and Events ... 82
- Traditional Folklore and Music ... 84
- Local Arts and Crafts ... 86
- Religious Sites and Pilgrimages ... 88
- Macedonian Cuisine and Wine Tasting ... 90

CHAPTER 8 ... 94
Outdoor Adventures ... 94
- Hiking and Trekking ... 94
- Rock Climbing and Mountaineering ... 96
- Skiing and Winter Sports ... 98
- River Rafting and Kayaking ... 100
- Wildlife and Nature Reserves ... 102

CHAPTER 9 ... 106
Practical Tips for Travelers ... 106
- Local Etiquette and Customs ... 106
- Health and Safety Precautions ... 108
- Communication and Internet Access ... 110
- Recommended Travel Apps ... 112

Useful Phrases in Macedonian...114
CONCLUSION AND ADDITIONAL RESOURCES **116**
RECAP OF MUST-SEE PLACES AND EXPERIENCES 116

Introduction to North Macedonia

Welcome to North Macedonia, a hidden gem nestled in the heart of the Balkans, where enchanting landscapes and captivating history converge to create a truly unforgettable experience for every traveler. Prepare to embark on a journey that will awaken your senses and leave an indelible mark on your soul. North Macedonia is a symphony of ancient traditions, breathtaking vistas, and warm-hearted hospitality, beckoning you to uncover its secrets and immerse yourself in its rich tapestry.

Imagine standing at the crossroads of East and West, where the past whispers its tales through ancient ruins and medieval monasteries. Here, history comes alive, inviting you to explore the timeless treasures that have withstood the test of time. Marvel at the imposing stone walls of Skopje Fortress, as it stands tall, a sentinel overlooking the vibrant capital city. Lose yourself amidst the intricate frescoes of the Church of St. John at Kaneo, perched on the shores of the mesmerizing Lake Ohrid, like a mystical beacon guiding your way.

As you traverse the winding streets of North Macedonia's cities and towns, prepare to be enchanted by the harmonious blend of cultures that have shaped this land. Skopje, the capital, is a living gallery, where Ottoman architecture rubs shoulders with gleaming modern structures, mirroring the nation's progressive spirit. Let your senses be tantalized by the aroma of traditional delicacies wafting from bustling bazaars, where locals gather to share stories and haggle over vibrant carpets, handmade crafts, and aromatic spices.

North Macedonia's natural beauty is an ode to the extraordinary diversity of the Balkan region. Picture yourself exploring the pristine shores of Lake Ohrid, its crystal-clear waters reflecting the surrounding mountains like a shimmering mirror. Dive into the depths of its underwater world, discovering hidden treasures and ancient artifacts. As the sun sets, casting hues of crimson and gold upon the tranquil lake, you'll be captivated by a sense of serenity that is simply unparalleled.

Venture beyond the captivating cities, and you'll be rewarded with landscapes that seem plucked from a fairytale. Lose yourself in the verdant embrace of Mavrovo National Park, where emerald forests give way to dramatic peaks and cascading waterfalls. Immerse yourself in the mystical allure of Matka Canyon, a hidden sanctuary of limestone cliffs, mysterious caves, and shimmering emerald waters. Embark on a journey to the ethereal world of Pelister National Park, where jagged mountain peaks pierce the sky, and alpine meadows come alive with a vibrant tapestry of wildflowers.

But North Macedonia's allure goes beyond its stunning vistas and awe-inspiring landscapes. It resides in the beating hearts of its people, who welcome visitors with open arms and share their traditions with genuine warmth. Engage in lively conversations with locals as you sip traditional rakija, a potent elixir that embodies the spirit of this land. Allow the melodies of Macedonian folk music to transport you to another time, where joyous celebrations bring communities together in harmonious unity.

Now, dear traveler, as your journey through North Macedonia begins, I implore you to open your heart to the wonders that await you. This guide will be your compass, leading you through the labyrinthine streets, ancient ruins, and breathtaking natural wonders that define this extraordinary country. Each page will unveil the hidden treasures and insider tips that will make your adventure all the more extraordinary.

So, fasten your seatbelt, dear wanderer, and get ready to delve into the remarkable tapestry of North Macedonia. From the enchanting allure of its cities to the untouched splendor of its natural landscapes, this journey will be etched in your memory forever. Prepare to be captivated, to be moved, and to fall deeply in love with the magic of North Macedonia. Your adventure awaits.

Chapter 1
Country Overview

North Macedonia, a landlocked country in the heart of the Balkan Peninsula, is a hidden gem waiting to be discovered by intrepid travelers. Bordered by Albania, Kosovo, Serbia, Bulgaria, and Greece, this small but remarkable nation offers a captivating blend of history, culture, and natural beauty.

With a population of approximately 2 million, North Macedonia is a melting pot of diverse ethnicities and rich traditions. The country's capital and largest city is Skopje, a vibrant metropolis where ancient landmarks harmoniously coexist with modern architecture. Skopje's grandeur is epitomized by the magnificent Stone Bridge, spanning the Vardar River, and the awe-inspiring statues that adorn its streets, reflecting the nation's deep-rooted heritage.

Beyond Skopje, North Macedonia reveals a myriad of treasures that will leave you spellbound. The UNESCO World Heritage-listed city of Ohrid, nestled on the shores of the breathtaking Lake Ohrid, is a cultural and natural haven. Its cobblestone streets wind through a labyrinth of medieval churches, ancient fortifications, and charming old houses, transporting you to a bygone era.

The country's landscapes are a testament to its natural diversity. From the rugged peaks of the Šar Mountains to the pristine lakes and lush forests of national parks like Mavrovo and Pelister, North Macedonia offers endless opportunities for outdoor enthusiasts and nature lovers. Whether you're hiking through scenic trails, sailing on tranquil lakes, or skiing down powdery slopes, the country's natural beauty will captivate your senses.

North Macedonia's rich history comes alive in its archaeological sites and cultural landmarks. The ancient city of Stobi reveals the remnants of Roman civilization, while the monastic complex of St. Naum showcases the country's religious heritage. Traditional Macedonian villages, such as Mavrovo and Kratovo, offer a glimpse into rural life and are adorned with distinctive architecture and charming hospitality.

The cuisine of North Macedonia is a delight for food lovers. Indulge in hearty traditional dishes like tavče gravče (baked beans), ajvar (roasted red pepper spread), and the famous pastrmajlija (flaky dough topped with marinated meat). Pair your meal with a glass of rakija, the local brandy, or sample regional wines that have been perfected over centuries.

When it comes to hospitality, North Macedonia's warm and welcoming people will make you feel like part of the family. They take pride in sharing their culture, traditions, and folklore with visitors, creating an immersive and authentic experience.

Geography and Climate

Geography: North Macedonia, although a small country, boasts diverse and captivating geography. Nestled in the central Balkan Peninsula, it is landlocked and bordered by five neighboring countries. The country is characterized by a varied topography that encompasses mountains, valleys, lakes, and rivers.

The dominant mountain range is the Šar Mountains, which stretch across the western part of the country. These majestic peaks offer breathtaking vistas and are a haven for outdoor enthusiasts, with opportunities for hiking, skiing, and mountaineering. The country is also home to other mountain ranges like the Osogovo, Bistra, and Jablanica, each with its own unique charm.

The interior of North Macedonia is marked by fertile valleys and picturesque plains, where agriculture thrives. The Vardar River, the country's longest and most important river, flows through the heart of North Macedonia, carving a path amidst the verdant landscapes.

One of the crown jewels of North Macedonia is Lake Ohrid, a UNESCO World Heritage site and one of the oldest and deepest lakes in Europe. The azure waters of Lake Ohrid are surrounded by stunning mountain ranges and are a haven for water-based activities, such as swimming, boating, and fishing.

Climate: North Macedonia experiences a transitional climate, influenced by Mediterranean, continental, and mountainous elements. The country's climate is characterized by hot, dry summers and cold winters, with significant regional variations.

In the lowland areas, summers are generally hot and dry, with temperatures often reaching above 30°C (86°F). Winters can be cold, especially in the mountainous regions, with temperatures dropping below freezing and snowfall common. Spring and autumn bring pleasant temperatures, making them ideal seasons for outdoor activities and exploring the natural beauty of the country.

The climate around Lake Ohrid is milder due to its proximity to the water, creating a more Mediterranean-like ambiance. Summers here are warm and humid, while winters are relatively mild compared to other parts of the country.

It's worth noting that North Macedonia's diverse topography can result in microclimates, where weather conditions can vary significantly within relatively short distances. Therefore, it's advisable to check the weather forecast for specific regions or consult locals for the most accurate information when planning outdoor activities.

Cultural Background

Cultural Background: North Macedonia is a tapestry of diverse cultural influences, shaped by its rich history and the fusion of various civilizations that have left their mark on the region. The cultural heritage of the country reflects a unique blend of Balkan, Mediterranean, and Eastern influences, resulting in a fascinating mosaic of traditions, customs, and artistic expressions.

The ancient kingdom of Macedon, ruled by Alexander the Great, serves as a cornerstone of North Macedonia's cultural legacy. The historical significance of the region is evident in archaeological sites like Stobi, Heraclea Lyncestis, and the ancient city of Ohrid. These sites offer a glimpse into the Hellenistic and Roman periods, showcasing the country's historical connections to the broader Mediterranean world.

The Byzantine era also played a crucial role in shaping North Macedonia's cultural identity. Numerous Byzantine churches and monasteries dot the landscape, adorned with magnificent frescoes and intricate architectural details. The iconic Church of St. Panteleimon in Ohrid and the Monastery of Saint Naum are prime examples of the country's Byzantine heritage.

During the Ottoman Empire's rule, North Macedonia experienced significant cultural and architectural influences. Mosques, hammams (bathhouses), and bazaars became integral parts of the urban fabric, particularly in cities like Skopje and Bitola. The Old Bazaar in Skopje, with its narrow cobblestone streets and Ottoman-era structures, stands as a testament to this period.

Folklore and traditional customs hold a special place in North Macedonian culture. The country is renowned for its vibrant traditional music, with lively rhythms and heartfelt melodies that evoke a sense of joy and celebration. Folk dances, such as the popular oro, are performed during festivals and social gatherings, reflecting the spirit and unity of the local communities.

Art and craftsmanship are cherished in North Macedonia, with a legacy of traditional crafts passed down through generations. Skilled artisans create intricate woodcarvings, handwoven textiles, and exquisite filigree jewelry, showcasing the country's artistic heritage.

Religion plays a significant role in North Macedonia's cultural fabric. The majority of the population adheres to Eastern Orthodox Christianity, with numerous churches and monasteries serving as important spiritual and cultural centers. Religious festivals, such as Easter and Christmas, are celebrated with great fervor and provide a window into the deeply rooted religious traditions of the country.

Hospitality is deeply ingrained in North Macedonian culture, and visitors are warmly welcomed. The locals take pride in sharing their customs, cuisine, and stories, ensuring that guests feel embraced and connected to the authentic essence of the country.

Chapter 2

Essential Travel Information

Entry Requirements and Visa

Entry Requirements

Valid passport: A valid passport is required for all visitors to North Macedonia. The passport must be valid for at least six months beyond the intended stay in North Macedonia.

Visa: Citizens of most countries do not need a visa to enter North Macedonia for tourist or business trips of less than 90 days within a six-month period. However, nationals of some countries, such as Afghanistan, Iran, and Pakistan, do need a visa to enter North Macedonia.

Proof of onward travel: Visitors must have proof of onward travel, such as a plane ticket or a bus ticket.

Health insurance: Visitors are not required to have health insurance to enter North Macedonia, but it is recommended.

Visa Requirements

Citizens of the following countries do not need a visa to enter North Macedonia for tourist or business trips of less than 90 days within a six-month period:

Albania

Andorra

Austria

Belgium

Bosnia and Herzegovina

Bulgaria

Croatia

Cyprus

Czech Republic

Denmark

Estonia

Finland

France

Germany

Greece

Hungary

Iceland

Ireland

Italy

Kosovo

Latvia

Liechtenstein

Lithuania

Luxembourg

Malta

Monaco

Montenegro

Netherlands

North Macedonia

Norway

Poland

Portugal

Romania

San Marino

Serbia

Slovakia

Slovenia

Spain

Sweden

Switzerland

Citizens of the following countries do need a visa to enter North Macedonia:

Afghanistan

Algeria

Bangladesh

China

Egypt

Iran

Iraq

Jordan

Kuwait

Lebanon

Libya

Morocco

Pakistan

Saudi Arabia

Sudan

Syria

Tunisia

United Arab Emirates

How to Apply for a Visa

If you need a visa to enter North Macedonia, you can apply for one at the nearest Macedonian embassy or consulate. You will need to provide the following documents:

A completed visa application form

A valid passport

Two recent passport-size photographs

Proof of onward travel

Proof of financial support

A visa fee

The visa application process can take several weeks, so it is important to apply well in advance of your travel date.

Customs

There are no restrictions on the amount of foreign currency that you can bring into North Macedonia. However, you must declare any amount over €10,000.

You are allowed to bring the following goods into North Macedonia without paying customs duty:

Personal belongings for your own use

200 cigarettes or 50 cigars or 100 grams of tobacco

2 liters of wine or 1 liter of spirits or 2 liters of beer

Gifts up to the value of €50

Pets

If you are bringing a pet into North Macedonia, you must have a valid health certificate from your veterinarian. The certificate must show that the pet has been vaccinated against rabies.

Further Information

For more information on entry requirements and visas for North Macedonia, please visit the website of the Macedonian Ministry of Foreign Affairs: https://www.mfa.gov.mk/

Currency and Money Matters

Currency and Money Matters: The official currency of North Macedonia is the Macedonian Denar (MKD). When planning your trip to North Macedonia, it's essential to familiarize yourself with the country's currency and understand how money matters are handled.

Currency Exchange: To obtain Macedonian Denars, you can exchange your foreign currency at banks, exchange offices (known as menjačnica), or authorized currency exchange booths. These facilities are widely available in cities and tourist areas. It's advisable to compare exchange rates and fees before making a transaction to ensure you get the best value for your money. Banks usually offer competitive rates, but exchange offices are convenient and easily accessible.

ATMs and Credit Cards: ATMs (Automated Teller Machines) are readily available in urban areas and major tourist destinations throughout North Macedonia. They accept major international debit and credit cards, allowing you to withdraw local currency. It's wise to check with your bank regarding any foreign transaction fees or withdrawal limits that may apply. Inform your bank of your travel plans to avoid any unexpected card issues.

Hotels, restaurants, and other major facilities accept credit cards like Visa and Mastercard widely. However, it's advisable to carry some cash, especially for smaller establishments, markets, or when traveling to more remote areas where card acceptance may be limited.

Tipping and Service Charges: Tipping in North Macedonia is appreciated but not obligatory. It's customary to leave a tip of around 10% for good service in restaurants, cafes, and bars. Some establishments may include a service charge on the bill, so check for this before adding an additional tip. Tipping hotel staff, tour guides, and taxi drivers is also customary, though not mandatory. Use your discretion and reward exceptional service accordingly.

Budgeting and Costs: North Macedonia offers excellent value for travelers, with prices generally being more affordable compared to other European countries. The cost of accommodation, meals, and transportation is reasonable, allowing you to explore and enjoy the country without breaking the bank.

However, it's always wise to have a rough budget in mind to manage your expenses effectively. Factors like the type of accommodation, dining preferences, and activities you choose can influence your overall expenditure. Research and plan ahead to get a sense of the average costs associated with your desired level of comfort and experiences.

Safety and Security: While North Macedonia is generally a safe destination, it's always advisable to take standard precautions to ensure the safety of your money and belongings. Keep your cash, cards, and important documents secure, use ATMs in well-lit and trusted locations, and be cautious of your surroundings when making transactions. It's a good idea to have a mix of payment options, including cash and cards, in case of any unforeseen circumstances.

Language and Communication

The official language of North Macedonia is Macedonian, and it is spoken by the majority of the population. Macedonian belongs to the South Slavic language group and has its own unique alphabet, known as Cyrillic. However, English is widely spoken and understood in tourist areas, hotels, restaurants, and among younger generations.

Here are some key points to keep in mind regarding language and communication in North Macedonia:

Macedonian Language: Learning a few basic phrases in Macedonian can greatly enhance your travel experience and facilitate interactions with locals. Here are some useful expressions:

Hello: Zdravo (ZDRAH-vo)

Thank you: Blagodaram (blah-GOH-dah-rahm)

Yes: Da (dah)

No: Ne (neh)

Excuse me/Pardon: Izvinete (iz-vee-NEH-teh)

Do you speak English?: Zboruvate li angliski? (zbo-ROO-vah-teh lee AHN-glees-kee?)

Goodbye: Doviduvanje (doh-vee-DOO-vahn-yeh)

English Language: English is commonly spoken in popular tourist destinations, hotels, and restaurants, especially in larger cities like Skopje and Ohrid. Many young people and those working in the tourism industry have a good command of English. However, it's still helpful to have a few basic Macedonian phrases or carry a phrasebook or translation app for situations where English may not be widely spoken.

Cyrillic Alphabet: The Macedonian language uses the Cyrillic alphabet, which may appear unfamiliar if you're accustomed to the Latin alphabet. Street signs, public transportation signs, and official documents are typically displayed in Cyrillic. Familiarizing yourself with the Cyrillic alphabet can be useful for navigating and understanding written information. However, many signs, especially in tourist areas, are often bilingual and also displayed in Latin script.

Signage and Information: In recent years, efforts have been made to include more bilingual signage, particularly in tourist areas. Maps, brochures, and informational materials are often available in multiple languages, including English.

Additionally, staff at tourist information centers are generally proficient in English and can provide assistance and guidance for your travels.

Non-Verbal Communication: Non-verbal communication, such as hand gestures and body language, can be helpful in overcoming language barriers. A friendly smile, nod, or simple gestures can convey basic messages and create a positive connection with locals.

Transportation within Macedonia

Transportation within North Macedonia offers several convenient options for travelers to explore the country's diverse landscapes and vibrant cities. Whether you're navigating urban areas or venturing into rural regions, here are the key modes of transportation to consider:

Bus: Buses are the primary mode of public transportation in North Macedonia, connecting major cities, towns, and even remote villages. The bus network is extensive and well-developed, making it a reliable and affordable option for travel. Skopje, the capital city, serves as a major transportation hub, with numerous bus lines operating from the central bus station. Look for reputable bus companies like Sloboda Prevoz, Ohridski Avtotransport, and Makpetrol for intercity journeys.

Train: North Macedonia's rail network connects several cities within the country, as well as international destinations like Belgrade (Serbia) and Thessaloniki (Greece). While the train service is not as extensive as the bus network, it offers a scenic and comfortable way to travel. The main railway station is located in Skopje, and tickets can be purchased at the station or online. It's advisable to check the train schedules in advance, as they may not operate as frequently as buses.

Car Rental: Renting a car provides the flexibility to explore North Macedonia at your own pace, especially if you plan to visit rural areas or less accessible attractions. Major international car rental agencies have offices in Skopje and Ohrid, offering a range of vehicles to suit your needs. The road infrastructure in North Macedonia is generally well-maintained, making self-driving a viable option. However, be aware that traffic rules and driving customs may differ from your home country, so exercise caution and familiarize yourself with local regulations.

Taxis: Taxis are widely available in urban areas and can be hailed on the street or booked through ride-hailing apps. Taxi fares in North Macedonia are relatively affordable, and it's recommended to ensure the driver uses the meter or agree on a fare before starting the journey. Registered taxis are usually marked with a "TAXI" sign and have a company logo displayed on the vehicle.

Shared Taxis and Minibuses: Shared taxis, known as "marshrutki" or "furgons," are a popular mode of transportation for shorter distances or between smaller towns. These minibus-like vehicles follow fixed routes and pick up passengers along the way. While they can be crowded, they offer a budget-friendly option for getting around and experiencing local transportation.

Domestic Flights: For longer distances or if you prefer air travel, domestic flights are available between Skopje and Ohrid. These flights are operated by the national carrier, Airports of North Macedonia (TAV Airports), and offer a quick and convenient way to travel between the two major cities.

Public Transportation

Bus: A one-way bus ticket within a city costs around 30 MKD (about $0.50 USD). A one-way bus ticket between cities costs around 500 MKD (about $8 USD).

Tram: A one-way tram ticket within Skopje costs around 20 MKD (about $0.30 USD).

Trolleybus: A one-way trolleybus ticket within Skopje costs around 20 MKD (about $0.30 USD).

Metro: The Skopje Metro is currently under construction, but when it is completed, a one-way metro ticket will cost around 20 MKD (about $0.30 USD).

Taxi: Taxis in North Macedonia are relatively inexpensive. A short taxi ride within a city costs around 100 MKD (about $1.50 USD). A taxi ride between cities costs around 500 MKD (about $8 USD).

Car Rental: Car rental in North Macedonia is also relatively inexpensive. A day's rental of a compact car costs around 50 EUR (about $55 USD).

Bicycle Rental: Bicycle rental is a popular option for getting around in North Macedonia. A day's rental of a bicycle costs around 10 EUR (about $11 USD).

Walking: Walking is a great way to get around in North Macedonia, especially in the smaller towns and villages.

Other: There are also a few other options for transportation in North Macedonia, such as intercity buses, shared taxis, and boats. The cost of these options will vary depending on the distance traveled and the type of transportation used.

Safety and Security Tips

Be aware of your surroundings: This is a general rule of thumb for any travel destination, but it is especially important in North Macedonia. Petty theft is the most common type of crime in the country, so it is important to be aware of your belongings and take precautions to protect them.

Don't flash your valuables: This is another common-sense tip, but it is worth repeating. Don't carry large amounts of cash or wear expensive jewelry in public. If you must bring valuables with you, keep them in a safe place, such as a hotel safe or a money belt.

Be careful at night: Nighttime is when crime rates tend to be higher, so it is best to avoid walking alone at night in unfamiliar areas. If you must walk at night, take a taxi or walk with a friend.

Be aware of scams: There are a few common scams that tourists should be aware of in North Macedonia. The "broken-down car" scam is a typical fraud. A person will approach you and tell you that their car has broken down and they need help. They may ask you to give them money or to help them push their car. If you encounter this scam, simply walk away.

Trust your instincts: If you feel unsafe in a situation, trust your instincts and leave. Don't be afraid to ask for help from a local or the police.

Here are some additional tips for staying safe in North Macedonia:

Stay informed about the latest security threats: The U.S. Department of State has a travel advisory for North Macedonia that provides information about current security threats. You can also sign up for email alerts from the State Department so that you will be notified of any changes to the travel advisory.

Learn some basic Macedonian phrases: This will help you communicate with locals and make it easier to get help if you need it.

Be respectful of local customs: North Macedonia is a conservative country, so it is important to be respectful of local customs. This entails acting modestly in public and avoiding demonstrations of affection.

Have fun! North Macedonia is a safe and beautiful country with a lot to offer visitors. Just be aware of your surroundings and take precautions to stay safe, and you're sure to have a great time.

Chapter 3

Planning Your Trip

Best Time to Visit

The best time to visit North Macedonia largely depends on your preferences and the activities you plan to engage in. The country experiences four distinct seasons, each offering its own unique charm and opportunities. Here's an overview of the different seasons to help you determine the best time for your visit:

Spring (April to June): Spring in North Macedonia brings mild temperatures, blooming landscapes, and an abundance of natural beauty. It's an excellent time to visit if you enjoy outdoor activities like hiking, exploring national parks, or strolling through picturesque towns. The temperatures during spring are pleasant, ranging from around 15°C to 25°C (59°F to 77°F), although they can vary depending on the altitude. Keep in mind that April and May might experience occasional rainfall, so pack a light rain jacket.

Summer (July to September): Summer is the peak tourist season in North Macedonia, offering warm to hot temperatures, especially in July and August. Temperatures can range from 25°C to 35°C (77°F to 95°F) in lower-lying areas, making it an ideal time for enjoying the country's stunning lakes, such as Lake Ohrid and Lake Prespa. Summer is also perfect for exploring vibrant cities like Skopje, attending outdoor festivals, and enjoying outdoor dining. Be prepared, nevertheless, for heavier crowds and more expensive lodging during this time.

Autumn (October to November): Autumn in North Macedonia brings mild and pleasant temperatures, ranging from around 10°C to 20°C (50°F to 68°F), making it an ideal time for cultural exploration and outdoor activities. The landscapes transform into a vibrant tapestry of autumnal colors, offering stunning photography opportunities. Autumn is also the harvest season, and you can experience local festivities and taste fresh produce at farmers' markets. However, note that November can be cooler and rainier, so layer your clothing and bring a light jacket.

Winter (December to February): Winter in North Macedonia is cold, particularly in mountainous regions, where snowfall is common. If you enjoy winter sports like skiing or snowboarding, the ski resorts of Mavrovo and Popova Shapka offer excellent opportunities. The temperatures in winter range from around -5°C to 5°C (23°F to 41°F) in lower-lying areas, but they can drop below freezing in mountainous regions. Winter also brings a festive atmosphere, with Christmas markets and cultural celebrations in cities like Skopje and Ohrid.

It's worth noting that North Macedonia's climate can vary across regions and altitudes, so consider the specific destinations you plan to visit when choosing the best time for your trip. Additionally, if you prefer fewer crowds and more affordable accommodation, consider visiting during the shoulder seasons of spring and autumn.

Duration of Stay

The ideal duration of stay in North Macedonia depends on your travel preferences, the destinations you plan to visit, and the experiences you wish to have. While it's possible to explore some of the country's highlights in a few days, a longer stay allows for a more immersive and comprehensive experience. Here are some considerations to help you determine the duration of your stay:

Short Visit (2-4 days): If you have limited time but still want to get a taste of North Macedonia, a short visit of 2-4 days can give you a glimpse of the country's main attractions. This timeframe allows you to explore the capital city, Skopje, with its impressive landmarks like the Stone Bridge and Skopje Fortress. You can also visit the beautiful town of Ohrid, a UNESCO World Heritage site known for its picturesque lake, historic sites, and stunning Orthodox churches. With a short visit, you'll have time for a few day trips or outdoor activities, such as hiking in Matka Canyon or visiting the charming town of Bitola.

Moderate Stay (5-7 days): With a moderate stay of 5-7 days, you can delve deeper into the cultural, historical, and natural wonders of North Macedonia. In addition to Skopje and Ohrid, you can explore other notable destinations like Bitola, known for its Ottoman architecture and bustling bazaar. The vibrant city of Tetovo offers a glimpse into the country's multicultural heritage, with its beautiful Painted Mosque and Arabati Baba Teke complex. Consider visiting the Mavrovo National Park, where you can enjoy outdoor activities such as hiking, skiing (in winter), and immersing yourself in the serene natural surroundings. This duration allows for a more relaxed pace and the opportunity to discover hidden gems off the beaten path.

Extended Stay (10+ days): For a truly immersive experience and a deeper exploration of North Macedonia's diverse regions, consider an extended stay of 10 days or more. With this timeframe, you can visit lesser-known destinations, such as the wine region of Tikveš or the enchanting town of Kratovo, famous for its ancient towers and traditional architecture. Explore the picturesque landscapes of the Pelister National Park or embark on a cultural journey through the Macedonian countryside, visiting traditional villages and monasteries. An extended stay provides the opportunity to attend local festivals, engage in cooking classes, or participate in outdoor activities like paragliding or horseback riding.

Choosing Your Destinations

Choosing your destinations in North Macedonia is an exciting part of trip planning, as the country offers a diverse range of attractions and experiences. Whether you're interested in historical sites, natural landscapes, cultural immersion, or a combination of everything, here are some destinations to consider when crafting your itinerary:

Skopje: As the capital city, Skopje is a vibrant hub of culture, history, and modern development. Marvel at the grand statues and architecture in the city center, including the iconic Alexander the Great statue and the Skopje Fortress. Visit the Old Bazaar, one of the largest and oldest bazaars in the Balkans, where you can explore narrow streets, shop for traditional crafts, and sample local cuisine.

Ohrid: Located on the shores of Lake Ohrid, the town of Ohrid is a UNESCO World Heritage site renowned for its natural beauty and rich history. Explore the well-preserved medieval architecture, such as the Church of St. John at Kaneo and the Ohrid Amphitheatre. Take a boat ride on Lake Ohrid to enjoy panoramic views of the town and visit the nearby St. Naum Monastery.

Bitola: Known as the "City of Consuls," Bitola is a charming town with a rich Ottoman and European architectural heritage. Stroll along Shirok Sokak, a pedestrian street lined with cafes, restaurants, and shops. Visit the Old Bazaar, explore the ruins of the ancient city of Heraclea Lyncestis, and enjoy the lively atmosphere of Bitola's cultural events.

Mavrovo National Park: Located in the western part of the country, Mavrovo National Park offers breathtaking mountain scenery, pristine lakes, and abundant wildlife. It's an ideal destination for outdoor enthusiasts, with opportunities for hiking, skiing, snowboarding, and wildlife spotting. Don't miss the enchanting Mavrovo Lake and the picturesque village of Galichnik.

Pelister National Park: Situated near the city of Bitola, Pelister National Park is a haven for nature lovers. The park is home to the highest peak in North Macedonia, Mount Pelister, offering stunning hiking trails, alpine meadows, and glacial lakes. Explore the diverse flora and fauna, including the rare Macedonian pine, and visit the iconic Big Lake and Small Lake.

Kratovo: Known as the "City of Towers," Kratovo is a small town famous for its well-preserved medieval architecture, stone bridges, and historic towers. Take a leisurely stroll through the winding streets, visit the Museum of Kratovo's History, and admire the unique stone-carved houses. Don't miss the chance to try the local specialty, "kratovska pita" (Kratovo pie).

Budgeting and Expenses

Accommodation: Hostels: $10-15 USD per night

Food: Restaurants: $5-10 USD per meal

Transportation: Public transportation: $1-2 USD per ride

Attractions: Entrance fees: $2-5 USD per attraction

Other: Souvenirs, alcohol, etc.: $5-10 USD per day

Total: $30-50 USD per day

Note: These are just average estimates, and your actual expenses may vary depending on your travel style and preferences.

Here is a more detailed breakdown of the different expenses you can expect to incur while traveling in North Macedonia:

Accommodation: There are a variety of accommodation options available in North Macedonia, from hostels to luxury hotels. Hostels are the most affordable option, with dorm beds starting at around $10 USD per night. Hotels range in price from around $20 USD to $100 USD per night.

Food: North Macedonian cuisine is a mix of Balkan and Mediterranean influences, and there are many delicious and affordable options available. You can get a good meal at a restaurant for around $5-10 USD. If you're on a tight budget, you can also find street food vendors selling everything from grilled meats to savory pastries for around $1-2 USD.

Transportation: Public transportation is the most affordable way to get around in North Macedonia. Buses and trams are the most common forms of public transportation, and tickets are very inexpensive. A car can also be rented, but the cost is higher.

Attractions: There are many historical and cultural attractions in North Macedonia, and entrance fees are generally very reasonable. You can expect to pay around $2-5 USD to enter most attractions.

Other: There are a few other expenses you may incur while traveling in North Macedonia, such as souvenirs, alcohol, and tips. Souvenirs are generally inexpensive, but you can easily spend more if you're not careful. Alcohol is also relatively inexpensive, with a beer costing around $1 USD and a glass of wine costing around $2 USD. Tips are not expected in North Macedonia, but you can tip if you feel the service was excellent.

Overall, North Macedonia is a very affordable country to travel to. You can easily get by on a budget of $30-50 USD per day, and you can even spend less if you're on a tight budget.

Here are some tips for budgeting your trip to North Macedonia:

Stay in hostels: Hostels are the most affordable option for accommodation in North Macedonia.

Prepare your own food: Preparing your own food is an excellent strategy to cut costs on food.

Take advantage of free activities: There are many free activities available in North Macedonia, such as visiting parks, hiking, and swimming.

Travel during the off-season: Traveling during the off-season is a great way to save money on flights and accommodation.

Packing Essentials

When preparing for your trip to North Macedonia, it's important to pack wisely and consider the specific needs and activities you'll engage in during your visit. Here are some essential items to include in your packing list:

Weather-Appropriate Clothing: Check the weather forecast for North Macedonia during your travel dates and pack clothing suitable for the season. Light and breathable clothes are ideal for summer, while warmer layers and a jacket are necessary for spring and autumn. In winter, pack warm winter clothing, including a coat, hat, gloves, and a scarf, especially if you plan to visit mountainous areas or engage in winter sports.

Comfortable Walking Shoes: Be prepared to explore cities, historical sites, and natural landscapes on foot. Comfortable walking shoes or sneakers are a must to ensure your feet remain comfortable during long walks and hikes. If you plan to engage in outdoor activities like hiking, consider packing a sturdy pair of hiking boots.

Travel Adapter: North Macedonia uses the European two-pin plug sockets, so make sure to bring a travel adapter to charge your electronic devices. This will allow you to conveniently use your phone, camera, and other gadgets without any compatibility issues.

Travel Documents: Carry your passport, visa (if required), and any other necessary travel documents in a secure and easily accessible place. It's also a good idea to keep digital copies of important documents, such as your passport and travel insurance, stored securely on your phone or in cloud storage.

Medications and First Aid Kit: If you take prescription medications, ensure you have an adequate supply for the duration of your trip. Additionally, pack a basic first aid kit with essentials like band-aids, pain relievers, antiseptic ointment, and any personal medications or medical supplies you may need.

Travel Insurance: It's highly recommended to have travel insurance that covers medical expenses, trip cancellation/interruption, and loss or theft of personal belongings. Check with your insurance provider to ensure you have sufficient coverage for your trip to North Macedonia.

Travel Guidebook or Map: Carry a travel guidebook or map of North Macedonia to help you navigate the country, learn about its history and culture, and discover hidden gems. Alternatively, you can use travel apps or offline maps on your smartphone for convenience.

Local Currency or Payment Methods: Carry some local currency (Macedonian denar) for small purchases, transportation, and emergencies. Ensure you have a mix of cash and payment methods like credit/debit cards, which are widely accepted in major establishments. It's also advisable to inform your bank about your travel plans to avoid any card-related issues.

Essential Toiletries and Personal Items: Pack travel-sized toiletries, including toothpaste, toothbrush, shampoo, conditioner, and any other personal care items you need.

Consider bringing sunscreen, insect repellent, and a reusable water bottle to stay hydrated during your explorations.

Language Guide or Translation App: While many people in North Macedonia speak English, carrying a language guidebook or using a translation app can be helpful for basic communication and understanding local customs.

Chapter 4

Exploring Skopje

Skopje City Overview

Skopje, the vibrant capital city of North Macedonia, is a captivating blend of old-world charm and modern aspirations. With its rich history, grand architecture, and lively atmosphere, Skopje offers a unique and immersive experience for visitors. Here's an overview of what you can expect when exploring Skopje:

Kale Fortress: Start your exploration by visiting the historic Kale Fortress, which dates back to the 6th century. This well-preserved fortress offers panoramic views of the city and the Vardar River. Take a leisurely stroll along its ancient walls and imagine the city's past as you admire the surrounding landscapes.

Macedonia Square and Stone Bridge: Head towards Macedonia Square, the city's central gathering place and a symbol of Skopje's grandeur. Here, you'll find the iconic statue of Alexander the Great, a powerful tribute to the country's historical heritage. Cross the nearby Stone Bridge, an architectural gem spanning the Vardar River, and soak in the vibrant atmosphere.

Old Bazaar (Stara Čaršija): One of the oldest and largest bazaars in the Balkans, the Old Bazaar is a must-visit destination in Skopje. Lose yourself in the labyrinthine streets lined with traditional shops, cafes, and Ottoman-era buildings. Browse through a wide array of handicrafts, carpets, spices, and jewelry, and savor local delicacies at charming traditional restaurants.

Skopje Fortress (Skopsko Kale): Perched on the hill overlooking the city, Skopje Fortress offers an intriguing glimpse into Skopje's past. Explore the ruins of this ancient fortress, which has witnessed centuries of history, and learn about the city's strategic significance. The fortress also hosts cultural events and concerts during the summer, providing a unique experience for visitors.

Mustafa Pasha Mosque: Admire the architectural beauty of the Mustafa Pasha Mosque, an exquisite example of Ottoman architecture. Step inside to appreciate its stunning interior adorned with intricate decorations and colorful tiles. The mosque's peaceful courtyard offers a serene escape from the bustling city streets.

Contemporary Skopje: Skopje's modern side is reflected in its striking architecture and contemporary landmarks. The city underwent an ambitious transformation in recent years, with new buildings and statues dotting its landscape. Marvel at the grandeur of the Macedonian Parliament, the

Archaeological Museum, and the Macedonian Opera and Ballet. Take a stroll across the futuristic Art Bridge and explore the vibrant City Park, a favorite spot among locals for leisurely walks.

Cultural and Artistic Heritage: Skopje is a city that celebrates its cultural and artistic heritage. Visit the Macedonian National Theater to enjoy a performance, explore the Macedonian Opera and Ballet, or discover the National Gallery of Macedonia, which houses a diverse collection of artworks. Skopje is also known for its numerous museums, including the Museum of Contemporary Art and the Memorial House of Mother Teresa.

Must-Visit Attractions

Skopje, the capital city of North Macedonia, is a treasure trove of attractions that cater to a variety of interests. From historical landmarks to cultural sites and architectural marvels, Skopje offers a plethora of must-visit attractions. Here are some highlights that should be on every visitor's itinerary:

Skopje Fortress (Kale): Perched on a hill overlooking the city, the Skopje Fortress, also known as Kale Fortress, is a symbol of Skopje's rich history. Explore its ancient walls, towers, and gates while enjoying panoramic views of the city below. The fortress is a fascinating testament to the city's strategic importance throughout the centuries.

Macedonia Square and Alexander the Great Statue: Macedonia Square is the heart of Skopje and home to the impressive statue of Alexander the Great, a prominent figure in Macedonian history. The statue is a striking sight, surrounded by grand neoclassical buildings and a lively atmosphere. This iconic landmark is a must-visit spot for history enthusiasts and photo opportunities.

Old Bazaar (Stara Čaršija): Step back in time as you wander through the vibrant Old Bazaar, one of the largest and oldest bazaars in the Balkans. Lose yourself in the narrow cobblestone streets lined with traditional shops, cafes, and hammams (Turkish baths). Immerse yourself in the lively atmosphere, haggle for unique souvenirs, and sample delicious Macedonian cuisine.

Stone Bridge (Kameni Most): Connecting the modern part of Skopje with the Old Bazaar, the Stone Bridge is an iconic landmark and a symbol of the city. This centuries-old bridge offers picturesque views of the Vardar River and serves as a gateway between the past and present. Stroll across the bridge and soak in the vibrant ambiance of Skopje.

Mother Teresa Memorial House: Visit the Mother Teresa Memorial House, dedicated to the life and humanitarian work of the famous Nobel Peace Prize laureate, Mother

Teresa. Explore the museum exhibits that showcase her life story and learn about her contributions to the world. The memorial house is a place of inspiration and reflection.

Church of St. Clement of Ohrid: Located in the heart of the Old Bazaar, the Church of St. Clement of Ohrid is an architectural masterpiece. Admire its stunning frescoes, intricate woodwork, and distinctive dome as you step inside this beautiful Orthodox church. The church holds historical and cultural significance for the Macedonian people.

Skopje City Park (Gradski Park): Escape the city bustle and relax in the tranquility of Skopje City Park. This green oasis offers lush gardens, walking paths, and recreational areas where you can unwind and enjoy nature. Take a leisurely stroll, have a picnic, or simply sit back and soak in the serene atmosphere.

Cultural and Historical Sites

Skopje is a treasure trove of cultural and historical sites that offer a glimpse into the rich heritage of the region. From ancient landmarks to architectural marvels and religious sites, here are some must-visit cultural and historical attractions in Skopje:

Skopje Fortress (Kale): Explore the ancient Skopje Fortress, perched on a hilltop overlooking the city. This historic landmark dates back to the 6th century and offers panoramic views of Skopje. Walk along its ancient walls, towers, and gates, and imagine the city's past as you soak in the captivating atmosphere.

Church of St. Clement of Ohrid: Go to the magnificent Orthodox Church of St. Clement of Ohrid, which is situated right in the middle of the Old Bazaar. Admire its beautiful frescoes, intricate woodwork, and ornate architecture. The church is dedicated to St. Clement of Ohrid, a medieval scholar and one of the most significant figures in Macedonian history.

Mustafa Pasha Mosque: Immerse yourself in Skopje's Ottoman heritage with a visit to the Mustafa Pasha Mosque. This elegant mosque, built in the 15th century, showcases exquisite Ottoman architecture and is one of the city's most iconic landmarks. Step inside to appreciate the mosque's intricate interior design and serene ambiance.

Skopje Old Bazaar (Stara Čaršija): Stroll through the historic Skopje Old Bazaar, one of the oldest and largest bazaars in the Balkans. This vibrant marketplace is a testament to Skopje's multicultural past, with influences from Ottoman, Byzantine, and Eastern European cultures. Discover traditional shops, admire Ottoman-era buildings, and sample local delicacies as you wander through its narrow cobblestone streets.

Museum of Macedonia: Delve into North Macedonia's history and culture at the Museum of Macedonia. This comprehensive museum showcases a diverse collection of artifacts, including archaeological finds, ethnographic exhibits, and art pieces. Learn about the country's ancient civilizations, traditional customs, and artistic heritage through its engaging displays.

Holocaust Memorial Center for the Jews of Macedonia: Pay homage to the memory of the Macedonian Jewish community at the Holocaust Memorial Center. This museum aims to preserve the memory of the Holocaust and educate visitors about the tragic events that unfolded during World War II. Explore the exhibits that document the history, culture, and suffering of the Macedonian Jews.

Millennium Cross: Venture outside the city center to witness the imposing Millennium Cross, perched atop the Vodno Mountain. This iconic landmark stands at a height of 66 meters (216 feet) and offers breathtaking panoramic views of Skopje and the surrounding landscapes. Take a cable car ride or hike to the cross for a memorable experience.

Shopping and Dining Recommendations

Shopping and dining in Skopje offer a delightful blend of traditional and modern experiences. Whether you're looking for unique souvenirs, exploring local markets, or indulging in mouthwatering Macedonian cuisine, Skopje has something for every visitor. Here are some shopping and dining recommendations to enhance your experience:

Shopping Recommendations:

Old Bazaar (Stara Čaršija): Explore the Old Bazaar, a vibrant marketplace brimming with shops, boutiques, and craftsmen offering a wide array of traditional goods. Browse through handmade carpets, intricate jewelry, traditional Macedonian costumes, and local handicrafts. Don't miss the Bit Pazar, a colorful open-air market where you can find fresh produce, spices, and local specialties.

Skopje City Mall: For a modern shopping experience, visit Skopje City Mall, one of the largest shopping centers in the region. This mall features a variety of international and local brands, along with entertainment options such as cinemas and restaurants. You'll find fashion, electronics, cosmetics, and more under one roof.

Gradski Trgovski Centar: Located in the city center, Gradski Trgovski Centar (City Shopping Center) is a popular destination for shopping enthusiasts. Explore the mall's multiple levels, which house a range of stores offering fashion, accessories, beauty products, and home goods.

Antique Shops: If you're a fan of antiques and unique collectibles, Skopje has several antique shops scattered throughout the city. These shops offer a treasure trove of vintage items, including furniture, books, coins, and artwork. Explore these hidden gems to discover a piece of history to take home.

Dining Recommendations:

Macedonian Traditional Cuisine: Indulge in the flavors of Macedonian cuisine by dining at traditional restaurants known as "kafanas". Sample local specialties such as tavče gravče (baked beans), ajvar (roasted red pepper spread), burek (savory pastry), and shopska salad (fresh salad with cheese). Don't forget to try Macedonian wines and rakija (fruit brandy) for a complete gastronomic experience.

Old Bazaar Eateries: While exploring the Old Bazaar, take a culinary journey by dining at one of the many authentic eateries. These establishments serve traditional Macedonian dishes alongside Middle Eastern and Turkish-inspired cuisine. Enjoy the atmospheric settings and savor local delicacies like kebabs, pita, and baklava.

Modern Restaurants and Cafes: Skopje also offers a vibrant contemporary dining scene, with a variety of international and fusion restaurants catering to different tastes. Discover trendy restaurants, rooftop bars, and stylish cafes offering a diverse range of cuisines, including Italian, Asian, Mediterranean, and more. Experience the fusion of flavors and enjoy the modern ambiance.

Street Food: For a quick and tasty bite, explore the street food scene in Skopje. Grab a slice of pastrmajlija (Macedonian pizza topped with meat), try traditional grilled meats from food stalls, or savor local pastries and desserts from street vendors. These flavorsome options provide a convenient and authentic taste of Skopje's culinary offerings.

Nightlife and Entertainment

When the sun sets in Skopje, the city comes alive with a vibrant nightlife and a range of entertainment options to suit every taste. From lively bars and clubs to cultural performances and live music venues, Skopje offers an exciting and diverse array of nighttime activities. Here are some recommendations for experiencing the nightlife and entertainment scene in Skopje:

Old Bazaar (Stara Čaršija): The Old Bazaar is not only a bustling marketplace during the day but also a hub of activity at night. Explore the narrow streets and discover charming cafes, bars, and pubs tucked away in historic buildings. Enjoy a laid-back evening with friends, sipping on local wines or trying craft beers while immersing yourself in the unique ambiance of this historic neighborhood.

Macedonia Square: Macedonia Square, with its grand architecture and iconic statues, transforms into a lively gathering place in the evening. Join locals and visitors alike as they take leisurely strolls, enjoy street performances, and revel in the vibrant atmosphere. The square is often host to cultural events, concerts, and festivals, providing a dynamic and entertaining experience.

Live Music Venues: Skopje boasts a vibrant live music scene, with various venues offering a range of genres to suit different tastes. From jazz clubs to rock bars and intimate acoustic settings, you can find live performances throughout the city. Check out popular venues such as MKC (Youth Cultural Center), Stanica 26, and Havana Summer Club for an evening of music and entertainment.

Cultural Performances: Immerse yourself in Skopje's cultural heritage by attending a traditional music or dance performance. The Macedonian Opera and Ballet, located in the city center, showcases world-class productions, including ballets, operas, and classical concerts. Additionally, the Macedonian Philharmonic Orchestra offers a diverse program of orchestral performances.

Bars and Nightclubs: Skopje offers a lively nightlife scene with a variety of bars and nightclubs catering to different preferences. Head to Debar Maalo, a neighborhood known for its vibrant bar scene, and explore the numerous establishments offering everything from cozy lounges to energetic dance floors. Club Epicentar and Club Sektor are popular choices for those seeking a night of dancing and electronic music.

Open-Air Summer Events: During the summer months, Skopje comes alive with open-air events and festivals. The City Park and the Skopje Fortress often host concerts, film screenings, and theater performances in picturesque outdoor settings. Keep an eye out for the Skopje Summer Festival, a month-long celebration of music, theater, and dance.

Casino Flamingo: If you're feeling lucky, try your hand at Casino Flamingo, one of Skopje's premier gaming establishments. Test your skills at the card tables, slot machines, or roulette wheels and enjoy the lively casino atmosphere. Even if you're not a gambler, the casino offers bars and entertainment options for a night out.

Chapter 5
Discovering Ohrid
Ohrid City Overview

Nestled on the shores of the magnificent Lake Ohrid, the city of Ohrid is a true gem of North Macedonia. With its stunning natural beauty, rich history, and vibrant cultural scene, Ohrid is a destination that captures the hearts of visitors from around the world. Let's explore the enchanting city of Ohrid.

Ohrid, often referred to as the "Jerusalem of the Balkans," is renowned for its historical significance and its picturesque setting. The city's origins date back over 2,000 years, making it one of the oldest human settlements in Europe. Its UNESCO World Heritage status is a testament to its exceptional cultural and natural importance.

As you arrive in Ohrid, you'll be captivated by the breathtaking views of Lake Ohrid, known for its crystal-clear waters and tranquil atmosphere. The lake is believed to be the oldest in Europe and is surrounded by rolling hills and majestic mountains, creating a stunning backdrop for the city.

Ohrid's rich history comes to life as you explore its narrow cobblestone streets and discover its numerous archaeological sites and ancient monuments. The city boasts over 365 churches, earning it the nickname "The City of Light". Admire the colorful frescoes that adorn the Byzantine-era churches, such as the famous Church of St. John at Kaneo, which is set on a rock above the lake.

The Ohrid Fortress, also known as Samuil's Fortress, is a testament to the city's medieval past. Climb its walls to enjoy panoramic views of the city, the lake, and the surrounding landscapes. Step back in time as you wander through its well-preserved ruins and imagine the ancient civilizations that once thrived within its walls.

Ohrid is also a center of learning and culture, home to the renowned Ohrid Literary School, which played a significant role in the development of Slavic literature and education. Visit the Ohrid Literary Museum to learn about the city's literary heritage and the contributions of its scholars.

The city's vibrant cultural scene comes alive during the Ohrid Summer Festival, a month-long celebration of music, dance, theater, and art. The festival attracts artists and performers from around the world, transforming Ohrid into a hub of creativity and entertainment.

Beyond its historical and cultural treasures, Ohrid offers a range of outdoor activities. Explore the lake by boat, swim in its pristine waters, or simply relax on the pebbled beaches. Hiking enthusiasts can venture into the nearby Galicica

National Park, where they can experience breathtaking views and discover diverse flora and fauna.

Ohrid's culinary scene is a delight for food lovers. Indulge in delicious Macedonian cuisine, characterized by its fresh ingredients, hearty flavors, and Balkan influences. Don't miss the opportunity to try Ohrid's famous trout, caught directly from Lake Ohrid and prepared in various mouthwatering ways.

As you wander through the streets of Ohrid, you'll encounter charming cafes, local artisans selling handicrafts, and lively markets offering traditional goods. Take a leisurely stroll along the lakeside promenade, soaking in the serene ambiance and the stunning sunset views.

Ohrid Lake and Natural Beauty

Ohrid Lake is a true natural wonder and one of the most mesmerizing features of the city of Ohrid. Known as the "Pearl of the Balkans," this ancient lake is a UNESCO World Heritage site and holds remarkable significance due to its unique ecology and geological history.

Stretching across the border of North Macedonia and Albania, Lake Ohrid is one of the deepest and oldest lakes in Europe, estimated to be around three million years old. Its crystal-clear waters shimmer with shades of emerald and azure, inviting visitors to immerse themselves in its refreshing embrace.

One of the most remarkable aspects of Lake Ohrid is its exceptional biodiversity. The lake is home to numerous endemic species found nowhere else on Earth, making it a living museum of evolution. Its pristine waters are inhabited by rare and protected species, including the Ohrid trout, which is cherished for its delicate taste.

Exploring Lake Ohrid is a delight for nature enthusiasts. Boat tours offer the opportunity to navigate the tranquil waters, providing stunning vistas of the surrounding mountains and the picturesque shoreline. Discover hidden coves, secluded beaches, and charming fishing villages as you sail across the calm surface.

For those seeking a bit of adventure, diving in Lake Ohrid is an extraordinary experience. The lake's crystal-clear waters allow for excellent visibility, revealing underwater landscapes adorned with submerged rocks, caves, and ancient relics. Dive into the depths to discover hidden treasures and encounter a diverse array of aquatic life.

The surrounding natural beauty of Lake Ohrid is equally captivating. The Galicica National Park, located on the slopes between Lake Ohrid and Lake Prespa, offers a sanctuary of unspoiled wilderness. Hiking trails wind through pristine forests, revealing panoramic views of the lake and the surrounding mountains.

Lake Ohrid also holds cultural significance, with several monasteries and churches perched along its shores. St. Naum Monastery, located on the southern end of the lake, is a must-visit destination. Explore the monastery complex, walk along the tranquil gardens, and witness the natural wonder of the "Ohrid Pearls" - freshwater pearls produced in Lake Ohrid.

As the sun sets over Lake Ohrid, the sky becomes a canvas for a breathtaking display of colors, casting a warm glow upon the water. Find a peaceful spot along the shoreline to witness this magical spectacle and allow yourself to be captivated by the serene beauty that surrounds you.

UNESCO World Heritage Sites

North Macedonia boasts several UNESCO World Heritage sites that reflect its rich history, cultural diversity, and outstanding universal value. These sites provide a glimpse into the country's fascinating past and showcase its contributions to art, architecture, and civilization. Here are some of the notable UNESCO World Heritage sites in North Macedonia:

Historic Center of Ohrid: The Historic Center of Ohrid, a UNESCO World Heritage site since 1980, is a treasure trove of historical and cultural significance. The city of Ohrid itself is a living museum, with its ancient churches, Byzantine-style architecture, and archaeological remains. Explore the iconic Church of St. Sofia, the stunning Church of St. John at Kaneo, and the ancient theater, which dates back to Hellenistic times.

Natural and Cultural Heritage of the Ohrid Region: The Ohrid Region was inscribed on the UNESCO World Heritage list in 1979 for its outstanding natural and cultural significance. This site encompasses both Lake Ohrid and the surrounding landscapes, which are home to unique flora and fauna. The region's cultural heritage is equally remarkable, with its medieval monasteries, archaeological sites, and traditional villages showcasing the rich history of the area.

Archaeological Site of Stobi: The Archaeological Site of Stobi, located near the town of Veles, was added to the UNESCO World Heritage list in 2017. Stobi was an ancient Roman city and an important crossroad between the east and west. Explore the remains of the theater, the basilicas, the ancient fortifications, and other structures that provide insight into the daily life of the Roman era.

Ancient City of Heraclea Lyncestis: The Ancient City of Heraclea Lyncestis, situated near the town of Bitola, is a significant archaeological site that was inscribed as a UNESCO World Heritage site in 2021. This site preserves the remains of an ancient Greek city founded by Philip II of Macedon, father of Alexander the Great. Discover the well-preserved theater, Roman baths, basilicas, and other structures that tell the story of this ancient city.

Water Activities and Beaches

Ohrid, with its stunning lake, offers a plethora of water activities and picturesque beaches that cater to both relaxation and adventure. Whether you seek tranquility on the shores or excitement on the water, Ohrid has something for everyone. Here are some water activities and beaches you can enjoy in Ohrid:

Swimming and Sunbathing: The clear and inviting waters of Lake Ohrid beckon visitors to take a refreshing dip. Enjoy a leisurely swim in the pristine lake, bask in the sun on the pebbled beaches, and unwind while admiring the breathtaking mountain views. Gradiste Beach and Kaneo Beach are popular choices for swimming and sunbathing, offering amenities such as loungers and parasols.

Boat Tours and Cruises: Embark on a boat tour or cruise to explore the beauty of Lake Ohrid from a different perspective. Discover hidden coves, secluded beaches, and charming lakeside villages as you sail across the calm waters.

Whether you opt for a relaxing sightseeing cruise or an adventure-packed speedboat tour, the boat excursions in Ohrid provide a memorable experience.

Kayaking and Canoeing: For those seeking a more active water adventure, kayaking and canoeing are excellent options. Rent a kayak or canoe and paddle along the tranquil waters of Lake Ohrid, discovering hidden bays and enjoying the serenity of the surrounding nature. It's a great way to explore the lake at your own pace and get closer to its pristine beauty.

Stand-Up Paddleboarding (SUP): Try your hand at stand-up paddleboarding (SUP) and experience a unique way of gliding across the calm surface of Lake Ohrid. Whether you're a beginner or an experienced SUP enthusiast, you can enjoy the peacefulness of the lake while engaging in a fun and rewarding activity. SUP rentals and lessons are available along the lakeshore.

Jet Skiing and Water Sports: For those seeking an adrenaline rush, jet skiing and other water sports are available on Lake Ohrid. Hop on a jet ski and feel the thrill as you speed across the water, or try your hand at water skiing, wakeboarding, or tubing for a memorable and exciting experience.

Fishing: Lake Ohrid is a haven for fishing enthusiasts. Join a fishing excursion or cast your line from the shore and try your luck at catching some of the lake's renowned trout. Fishing in Lake Ohrid not only offers the opportunity to engage in a relaxing and meditative activity but also provides a chance to savor the region's culinary specialty.

Sunset Cruises: End your day in Ohrid with a romantic sunset cruise on Lake Ohrid. Witness the sky ablaze with colors as the sun sets behind the mountains, casting a magical glow over the water. Relax on the boat, sip on a refreshing drink, and soak in the serene beauty of the surroundings.

Local Cuisine and Traditional Crafts

Ohrid not only captivates visitors with its stunning natural beauty and rich history but also entices with its delectable local cuisine and vibrant traditional crafts. Exploring the city's culinary scene and traditional crafts is a delightful way to immerse yourself in the local culture. Here are some highlights of Ohrid's cuisine and traditional crafts:

Local Cuisine: Ohrid's culinary offerings showcase a blend of Balkan, Mediterranean, and Ottoman influences, resulting in a diverse and flavorful cuisine. Here are some must-try dishes and culinary experiences in Ohrid:

Ohrid Trout: As a city situated on Lake Ohrid, it comes as no surprise that Ohrid trout is a local specialty. This delicious freshwater fish is known for its delicate flavor and tender flesh. Try it grilled, fried, or stuffed with aromatic herbs for a mouthwatering culinary experience.

Tavche Gravche: Tavche Gravche is a traditional Macedonian dish that consists of baked beans prepared in a clay pot. The slow cooking process enhances the flavors, resulting in a rich and hearty vegetarian dish. It is often served with a side of fresh bread and a dollop of creamy kaymak.

Ajvar: Ajvar is a popular condiment made from roasted red peppers, eggplant, garlic, and spices. It is a flavorful accompaniment to various dishes, including grilled meats, sandwiches, and bread. Don't miss the opportunity to savor this delicious and versatile sauce during your visit.

Shopska Salad: Indulge in a refreshing Shopska salad, a staple in Macedonian cuisine. This colorful salad combines fresh tomatoes, cucumbers, peppers, onions, and grated sirene cheese. It is drizzled with olive oil and sprinkled with aromatic herbs, making it a delightful and healthy choice.

Local Wines: North Macedonia has a long-standing tradition of winemaking, and Ohrid is no exception. Sample the region's excellent wines, including the indigenous Vranec and Stanushina grape varieties. Take a tour of local wineries to learn about the winemaking process and enjoy wine tastings with picturesque views.

Traditional Crafts: Ohrid is known for its skilled artisans and the preservation of traditional craftsmanship. Exploring the city's traditional crafts allows you to appreciate the artistic heritage and take home unique souvenirs. Here are some traditional crafts to discover in Ohrid:

Filigree Jewelry: Filigree jewelry is a traditional craft that involves intricate metalwork and delicate designs. Explore local jewelry shops to find beautifully crafted earrings, necklaces, and bracelets made using this ancient technique. These pieces make for exquisite and meaningful keepsakes.

Wood Carving: Wood carving is deeply rooted in Ohrid's heritage. Visit local workshops and witness master craftsmen transform blocks of wood into intricately carved sculptures, furniture, and decorative items. You can find exquisite wooden souvenirs that showcase the city's artistic craftsmanship.

Embroidery: Embroidery is a cherished tradition in North Macedonia, and Ohrid is known for its fine embroidery work. Discover embroidered textiles, including tablecloths, pillow covers, and traditional costumes, adorned with intricate patterns and vibrant colors. These handcrafted items reflect the region's cultural heritage.

Pottery: Ohrid's pottery tradition dates back centuries, and the city is famous for its unique ceramic creations. Visit pottery studios to witness skilled potters shaping clay into exquisite vases, bowls, and decorative items. Bring home a piece of Ohrid's pottery as a beautiful reminder of your visit.

Chapter 6

Venturing into Other Regions

Matka Canyon

Matka Canyon is a natural gem nestled just a short distance from Skopje, the capital city of North Macedonia. This awe-inspiring destination is a haven for nature enthusiasts, adventure seekers, and those seeking tranquility amidst breathtaking landscapes. Matka Canyon offers a myriad of attractions and activities that promise an unforgettable experience. Here's what you can expect when visiting Matka Canyon:

Spectacular Scenery: Prepare to be mesmerized by the stunning natural beauty of Matka Canyon. Towering cliffs, rugged rock formations, and lush greenery surround the winding Matka River, creating a picturesque backdrop that seems straight out of a fairytale. The crystal-clear waters of the river reflect the vibrant colors of the surrounding flora, adding to the enchanting atmosphere.

Boat Tours: Embark on a boat tour along the Matka River to fully immerse yourself in the canyon's splendor. Glide through the calm waters, passing by towering cliffs and hidden caves. Marvel at the abundance of wildlife, including various bird species that call the canyon home. The boat tours provide a peaceful and scenic way to explore the canyon's nooks and crannies.

Cave Exploration: Matka Canyon is renowned for its network of caves, which beckon adventurers to delve into their mysteries. Vrelo Cave, the deepest underwater cave in Europe, is a must-visit highlight. Take a guided tour to witness the enchanting stalactites, stalagmites, and underground lakes within the cave. The experience is truly captivating and offers a glimpse into the hidden wonders of the earth.

Hiking and Nature Trails: For outdoor enthusiasts, Matka Canyon offers a plethora of hiking and nature trails. Lace up your hiking boots and venture into the canyon's trails, which wind through forests, along the river, and up the surrounding hills. Enjoy panoramic views of the canyon, discover hidden waterfalls, and encounter the rich biodiversity that thrives in this pristine natural environment.

Rock Climbing and Canyoneering: Matka Canyon is a paradise for rock climbing and canyoneering enthusiasts. The steep cliffs and rugged terrain provide an ideal playground for these thrilling activities. Challenge yourself to ascend the cliffs or descend into the canyon's depths with the guidance of experienced instructors. It's an adrenaline-fueled adventure that allows you to fully appreciate the canyon's raw beauty.

St. Andrew's Monastery: Located within Matka Canyon, St. Andrew's Monastery is a significant historical and religious site. The monastery, perched on a cliff overlooking the canyon, offers a serene and spiritual ambiance. Explore the monastery complex, admire its frescoes, and take in the panoramic views from its vantage point. It's a peaceful retreat within the captivating surroundings of Matka Canyon.

Mavrovo National Park

Nestled in the western part of North Macedonia, Mavrovo National Park is a paradise for nature lovers and outdoor enthusiasts. Spanning over 73,000 hectares, this expansive and diverse national park offers breathtaking landscapes, pristine wilderness, and a wide array of activities for visitors to enjoy. Here's what you can expect when exploring Mavrovo National Park:

Majestic Mountains: Mavrovo National Park is characterized by its majestic mountain ranges, the most prominent being Mount Bistra. The towering peaks, rugged cliffs, and lush valleys create a dramatic backdrop for outdoor adventures. The park is a haven for hikers, mountaineers, and photographers seeking awe-inspiring views and the thrill of conquering the peaks.

Lake Mavrovo: Lake Mavrovo, the largest artificial lake in North Macedonia, is a centerpiece of the national park.

Surrounded by forested slopes and picturesque landscapes, the lake offers a tranquil setting for relaxation and recreational activities. Enjoy a leisurely boat ride, go fishing, or simply soak in the serene beauty of the lake and its surroundings.

Hiking and Trekking: Mavrovo National Park boasts an extensive network of hiking and trekking trails, catering to all levels of experience and fitness. From leisurely walks through meadows and forests to challenging mountain ascents, there's a trail for everyone. Explore the diverse flora and fauna, discover hidden waterfalls, and revel in the serenity of nature.

Skiing and Winter Sports: During the winter months, Mavrovo National Park transforms into a snowy wonderland, attracting winter sports enthusiasts from near and far. The park features a ski center with well-groomed slopes suitable for skiers and snowboarders of all levels. Enjoy the thrill of gliding down the slopes, try cross-country skiing, or indulge in snowshoeing amidst the pristine winter landscapes.

Biodiversity and Wildlife: Mavrovo National Park is home to a rich biodiversity, including numerous plant and animal species. Explore the park's diverse ecosystems, ranging from dense forests to alpine meadows, and keep an eye out for rare and endemic species. If you're lucky, you may spot

Balkan chamois, brown bears, wolves, or the elusive Balkan lynx, which is one of the rarest cat species in the world.

Cultural Heritage: Beyond its natural wonders, Mavrovo National Park is also steeped in cultural heritage. Explore the traditional villages scattered throughout the park, where you can witness the traditional way of life and admire the unique architecture. Don't miss the opportunity to visit the picturesque St. Jovan Bigorski Monastery, renowned for its exquisite frescoes and serene setting.

Bitola and Pelister National Park

Bitola, known as the "City of Consuls," and its neighboring Pelister National Park are must-visit destinations in North Macedonia. Bitola is a city rich in history and culture, while Pelister National Park boasts breathtaking natural landscapes and outdoor activities. Here's what you can expect when exploring Bitola and Pelister National Park:

Bitola:

Historical Significance: Bitola is a city steeped in history, with a legacy that dates back to ancient times. Explore the city's vibrant past as you stroll through its charming streets lined with neoclassical buildings, Ottoman-era mosques, and grand consulates. Don't miss the opportunity to visit the famous Heraclea Lyncestis archaeological site, where you can marvel at ancient ruins and well-preserved mosaics.

Shirok Sokak: Shirok Sokak, the city's main pedestrian street, is a bustling hub of activity. Lined with cafes, restaurants, and shops, it offers a vibrant atmosphere and a chance to experience Bitola's local culture. Enjoy a leisurely walk, savor traditional Macedonian cuisine, and indulge in shopping for unique souvenirs.

Bezisten: Bezisten, an Ottoman-era covered market, is a hidden gem in Bitola. This historical building houses numerous shops and artisans, offering traditional crafts, handmade items, and local products. Explore the labyrinthine corridors, admire the craftsmanship, and take home a piece of Bitola's cultural heritage.

Pelister National Park:

Majestic Peaks: Pelister National Park is renowned for its majestic mountain peaks, most notably Mount Pelister itself. Towering at over 2,601 meters, it offers breathtaking panoramic views of the surrounding landscapes. Embark on a challenging hike to the summit, where you'll be rewarded with sweeping vistas of lush forests, glacial lakes, and neighboring mountain ranges.

Outdoor Activities: Pelister National Park is a paradise for outdoor enthusiasts. From hiking and trekking to mountain biking and paragliding, there's an array of activities to suit every adventure seeker. Explore the park's well-marked trails, encounter diverse flora and fauna, and breathe in the fresh mountain air as you immerse yourself in the park's natural beauty.

Prespa Lakes: Located near Pelister National Park, the Prespa Lakes are a stunning natural treasure shared between North Macedonia, Albania, and Greece. These interconnected lakes are teeming with biodiversity, making them a haven for birdwatching enthusiasts. Spot rare and endangered bird species as you navigate the tranquil waters, or simply relax by the lakeside and admire the serene surroundings.

Skiing and Snowboarding: During the winter months, Pelister National Park transforms into a winter sports playground. The park features a ski center with well-groomed slopes suitable for skiers and snowboarders of all levels. Enjoy the thrill of gliding down the snowy slopes, surrounded by picturesque winter landscapes.

Kratovo and Kuklica Stone Dolls

Kratovo and the Kuklica Stone Dolls are two remarkable destinations in North Macedonia that offer a blend of history, natural beauty, and intriguing legends. Let's dive deeper into these captivating places:

Kratovo: Nestled in the scenic landscape of northeastern North Macedonia, Kratovo is a town that transports you back in time. Its cobblestone streets, Ottoman-era architecture, and rich cultural heritage make it a delight to explore. Here's what you can expect in Kratovo:

Ancient Origins: Kratovo has a long and storied history dating back to ancient times. As you wander through its narrow streets, you'll encounter well-preserved historical buildings, arches, and bridges that harken back to its past as a medieval mining town.

Medieval Towers and Clock Tower: The town is famous for its medieval towers, which were once defensive structures. The impressive Tower of Vukashin and the Saraj Tower are architectural gems that offer panoramic views of the town and its surroundings. Don't miss the opportunity to climb the Clock Tower, locally known as Saat Kula, and enjoy stunning vistas.

Underground Labyrinths: Kratovo is known for its intricate underground tunnels and labyrinths, remnants of its mining history. These tunnels, often referred to as "dolap," were used to extract minerals like silver and lead. Exploring these underground passages provides a fascinating glimpse into the town's mining heritage.

Kuklica Stone Dolls: Just a short distance from Kratovo, you'll find the mesmerizing phenomenon of the Kuklica Stone Dolls. These natural rock formations, scattered across a hillside, resemble human figures and carry with them a sense of mystery. Here's what makes the Kuklica Stone Dolls so intriguing:

Geological Marvel: The Kuklica Stone Dolls are the result of centuries of natural erosion and weathering. These unique rock formations have taken on shapes that resemble human figures, each with its distinct characteristics and stories.

Legends and Folklore: The Kuklica Stone Dolls are steeped in local legends and folklore. According to one popular story, these stone figures are the result of a doomed wedding ceremony. The dolls are said to represent petrified wedding guests, frozen in stone for eternity.

Scenic Beauty: The Kuklica Stone Dolls are set against a backdrop of scenic beauty, with rolling hills and breathtaking vistas. As you explore the area, take in the panoramic views and marvel at the natural wonders that surround these enigmatic stone figures.

Stobi Archaeological Site

The Stobi Archaeological Site, nestled in the heart of North Macedonia, is a treasure trove of ancient history and a testament to the region's rich cultural heritage. As you step foot into this captivating site, prepare to be transported back in time to the days of the Roman Empire and beyond. Here's what you can expect when exploring the Stobi Archaeological Site:

Ancient Roman City: Stobi was once a thriving Roman city, strategically located on the crossroads between the east and west. As you wander through the site, you'll encounter remarkably preserved ruins that showcase the grandeur of Roman architecture and urban planning. Explore the remnants of the theater, basilicas, temples, and residential buildings, and imagine life in this bustling city centuries ago.

Mosaic Splendors: Stobi is renowned for its exquisite mosaics, which have survived the test of time and continue to captivate visitors. Marvel at the intricate designs and vibrant colors of these ancient artworks, which depict scenes from mythology, daily life, and the Roman world. The House of the Psalms and the House of Peristeria are particular highlights where you can witness the beauty of these mosaic masterpieces.

Early Christian Heritage: Beyond its Roman legacy, Stobi also played a significant role in the early Christian period. Explore the remains of early Christian churches and witness the fusion of Roman architectural elements with Christian symbolism. The Episcopal Basilica, with its stunning floor mosaics and intricate stone carvings, stands as a testament to this fascinating era.

Ancient Theater: The ancient theater of Stobi is a true architectural gem. Built in the 2nd century, this well-preserved amphitheater once hosted theatrical performances and other public gatherings. Imagine the echoes of ancient applause as you stand amidst the grand seating area and take in the panoramic view of the stage and surrounding landscape.

Archeological Museum: The Stobi Archaeological Site is complemented by an on-site museum that provides further insights into the rich history and artifacts discovered at the site. Explore the museum's collection of sculptures, pottery, jewelry, and other artifacts, which offer a deeper understanding of the daily life and culture of the people who once inhabited Stobi.

Chapter 7
Cultural Experiences

Macedonian Festivals and Events

Macedonia, with its rich cultural heritage and vibrant traditions, offers a plethora of festivals and events throughout the year. These celebrations provide a unique opportunity to immerse yourself in the local culture, witness traditional customs, and experience the infectious enthusiasm of the Macedonian people. Here are some of the most notable festivals and events in Macedonia:

Ohrid Summer Festival (Ohrid, July-August): This internationally acclaimed festival takes place in the picturesque city of Ohrid during the summer months. It features a diverse program of music, dance, theater, and art performances, showcasing both local and international talent. The festival's enchanting atmosphere and stunning venues, including the ancient theater and churches, make it a must-attend event.

Skopje Jazz Festival (Skopje, October): Jazz enthusiasts flock to Skopje for this renowned festival that celebrates the genre's improvisational spirit and creativity. The festival hosts world-class musicians who take the stage to deliver captivating performances across various jazz styles. Prepare to be enthralled by the soulful sounds and energetic rhythms that fill the air.

Galicnik Wedding (Galicnik, July): The Galicnik Wedding is a unique cultural event that showcases the traditional Macedonian wedding customs. The picturesque village of Galicnik comes alive with music, dance, and vibrant celebrations. Visitors have the chance to witness the elaborate wedding ceremonies, traditional folk dances, and taste delicious local cuisine.

Taksirat Festival (Skopje, June): Taksirat Festival is a celebration of alternative and indie music, bringing together local and international artists for a series of concerts and performances. The festival creates a dynamic and electric atmosphere, attracting music lovers of all ages. Immerse yourself in the sounds of emerging talents and established artists in a setting that exudes creativity.

Balkan Folklore Festival (Bitola, July): This festival showcases the rich tapestry of Balkan folklore and traditional dance. Folk dance groups from Macedonia and other Balkan countries come together to perform vibrant and intricate routines, showcasing their cultural heritage through captivating performances. Experience the energy and rhythm of traditional Balkan music and witness the colorful traditional costumes.

Vevcani Carnival (Vevcani, January): Held annually in the village of Vevcani, this unique carnival is known for its vibrant and satirical atmosphere. Participants don eccentric costumes and masks, and the streets come alive with music, dance, and humorous performances. The carnival is a celebration of Macedonian folklore, culture, and a platform for social and political commentary.

Traditional Folklore and Music

Macedonia is a land deeply rooted in its folklore and traditional music, offering a captivating glimpse into the country's cultural heritage. The vibrant rhythms, heartfelt melodies, and lively dances of Macedonian folklore have been passed down through generations, creating a rich tapestry of traditional music and dance. Here's an exploration of traditional folklore and music in Macedonia:

Folk Music: Macedonian folk music is characterized by its distinct rhythms, haunting melodies, and rich vocal harmonies. Instruments like the gaida (bagpipe), kaval (wooden flute), zurla (double-reed instrument), tambura (long-necked lute), and tapan (drum) create a unique and enchanting sound. The lyrics often revolve around themes of love, nature, and historical events, reflecting the cultural identity of the Macedonian people.

Oro Dance: The oro is a traditional Macedonian circle dance that holds great significance in the country's folklore. It is performed during various celebrations, such as weddings, festivals, and cultural events. The dancers join hands and move in a rhythmic circular pattern, creating a sense of unity and community. The oro is not only a joyous dance but also a symbol of Macedonian identity and cultural pride.

Folklore Costumes: Macedonian folklore costumes are a visual representation of the country's cultural diversity and regional traditions. Each region has its unique style of costume, characterized by colorful fabrics, intricate embroidery, and ornate jewelry. These costumes are often worn during festive occasions and cultural events, adding to the vibrant atmosphere and reflecting the pride in Macedonian heritage.

Traditional Instruments: Traditional instruments play a vital role in Macedonian folklore music. The gaida, with its distinctive sound, is considered the national instrument of Macedonia and is often featured prominently in folk ensembles. Other instruments like the kaval, zurla, tambura, and tapan contribute to the rich and diverse soundscape of Macedonian traditional music.

Folk Festivals and Competitions: Throughout the year, various folk festivals and competitions take place across Macedonia, showcasing the country's vibrant folklore and traditional music. These events bring together folk dance groups, music ensembles, and singers from different regions, providing a platform to preserve and celebrate Macedonian cultural heritage. The festivals offer a fantastic opportunity to witness authentic performances and experience the infectious energy of Macedonian folklore firsthand.

Vocal Traditions: Macedonia is also renowned for its unique vocal traditions, such as the polyphonic singing style known as "acapella". This mesmerizing technique involves multiple singers harmonizing together without the accompaniment of musical instruments. The result is a captivating and harmonious blend of voices that echoes the soulful spirit of Macedonian folk music.

Local Arts and Crafts

Macedonia boasts a rich tradition of local arts and crafts, with skilled artisans preserving age-old techniques and creating unique handmade treasures. Exploring the world of Macedonian arts and crafts is an opportunity to witness the creativity, craftsmanship, and cultural heritage of the country. Here are some of the notable arts and crafts that you can discover in Macedonia:

Woodcarving: Woodcarving is deeply ingrained in Macedonian culture and craftsmanship. Skilled artisans carve intricate designs and patterns into wood, creating stunning pieces of art and functional objects. Look out for beautifully carved wooden chests, furniture, decorative panels, and utensils that showcase the mastery of the local woodcarvers.

Filigree Jewelry: Filigree jewelry holds a special place in Macedonian traditional craftsmanship. Delicate and ornate, filigree pieces are created by expert silversmiths who meticulously shape and intertwine silver or gold wires into intricate patterns. The result is exquisite jewelry pieces, including necklaces, earrings, bracelets, and rings, that reflect the timeless beauty of Macedonian filigree artistry.

Pottery and Ceramics: Pottery and ceramics have a long history in Macedonia, dating back to ancient times. Skilled potters continue to produce unique clay vessels, plates, bowls, and decorative items using traditional techniques. Look for hand-painted ceramics adorned with vibrant colors and intricate patterns that capture the essence of Macedonian pottery traditions.

Embroidery: Embroidery is a cherished craft in Macedonia, with women often passing down their stitching skills through generations. Traditional Macedonian embroidery features intricate patterns and vibrant colors, adorning traditional costumes, home decor items, and accessories like bags and tablecloths. The attention to detail and the rich symbolism within the embroidery reflect the cultural significance of this craft.

Iconography: Macedonia has a long-standing tradition of religious iconography, with skilled artists meticulously painting icons that are revered as sacred objects. These icons, often found in churches and monasteries, are characterized by their intricate brushwork, vibrant colors, and spiritual significance. They serve as visual representations of faith and are cherished for their artistic and religious value.

Carpets and Textiles: Macedonian carpets and textiles exhibit a blend of traditional motifs, patterns, and colors. Skilled weavers create intricate rugs and textiles using traditional looms, resulting in pieces that showcase the region's unique aesthetic. These carpets and textiles are not only functional but also serve as works of art that reflect the cultural identity of Macedonia.

Religious Sites and Pilgrimages

Macedonia is a country with a rich religious heritage, where ancient traditions and spiritual practices coexist. It is home to various religious sites and pilgrimage destinations that hold deep significance for locals and visitors alike. Whether you are seeking spiritual enlightenment, historical insights, or architectural marvels, exploring Macedonia's religious sites and embarking on pilgrimages is a truly enriching experience. Here are some notable religious sites and pilgrimage destinations in Macedonia:

Ohrid and Its Monasteries: The city of Ohrid, a UNESCO World Heritage site, is renowned for its spiritual and cultural significance. It houses several monasteries, including the iconic St. Naum Monastery, St. Panteleimon Monastery, and St. John at Kaneo Church. These monastic complexes not only showcase remarkable architectural beauty but also offer a tranquil atmosphere for contemplation and prayer.

St. Jovan Bigorski Monastery: Nestled in the scenic mountains of western Macedonia, the St. Jovan Bigorski Monastery is a must-visit destination for religious pilgrims. Known for its striking white facade, intricate wood-carved iconostasis, and serene surroundings, this monastery offers a peaceful retreat for spiritual reflection and worship.

Holy Mother of God Peribleptos Church: Located in Ohrid, the Holy Mother of God Peribleptos Church is an architectural gem that showcases Byzantine influences. Admire its stunning frescoes and iconography that depict biblical scenes and saints. The church stands as a testament to the rich religious heritage of Macedonia.

St. Clement of Ohrid Church: Situated in the heart of Skopje, the capital city, St. Clement of Ohrid Church is an important Orthodox Christian site. With its striking architecture, ornate interior, and religious artifacts, the church serves as a symbol of spiritual devotion and cultural identity.

Arabati Baba Teke: For those interested in Sufi mysticism and Islamic heritage, a visit to the Arabati Baba Teke in Tetovo is a must. This unique complex houses a dervish lodge, mosque, and other religious structures. Experience the tranquility of the surroundings and witness the spiritual practices of the local Sufi community.

Monastery of St. Joachim Osogovski: Nestled in the lush forests of the Osogovo Mountains, the Monastery of St. Joachim Osogovski is a significant Orthodox Christian pilgrimage site. The monastery's beautiful frescoes, stunning iconography, and peaceful ambiance make it a spiritual haven for both pilgrims and visitors seeking a serene retreat.

Holy Transfiguration Monastery (Crna Reka): Located in the scenic Pelagonia region, the Holy Transfiguration Monastery is a place of pilgrimage for Orthodox Christians. Surrounded by natural beauty, the monastery is renowned for its healing waters and is visited by believers seeking spiritual solace and physical well-being.

Macedonian Cuisine and Wine Tasting

Macedonian cuisine is a delightful blend of flavors, influenced by the country's geographical location and cultural diversity. From hearty traditional dishes to delectable desserts, Macedonian cuisine offers a range of culinary delights that will satisfy every palate. Additionally,

Macedonia is gaining recognition as a wine-producing region, with vineyards that produce high-quality wines. Here's a glimpse into the world of Macedonian cuisine and wine tasting:

Traditional Macedonian Dishes: a. Tavče Gravče: This is Macedonia's national dish, a hearty and comforting meal consisting of beans cooked in a clay pot with various spices and herbs. b. Ajvar: A delicious roasted red pepper and eggplant relish, often served as a condiment or spread. c. Šopska Salad: A refreshing and colorful salad made with tomatoes, cucumbers, peppers, onions, and grated white cheese. d. Sarma: Cabbage leaves stuffed with a flavorful mixture of minced meat, rice, and herbs, simmered in a savory tomato sauce. e. Pastrmajlija: A traditional Macedonian pizza-like dish topped with marinated and fried cubes of meat, onions, and peppers. f. Kebapi: Grilled sausages made from minced meat, usually served with fresh bread and ajvar.

Macedonian Desserts: a. Tulumba: Deep-fried sweet pastry strips soaked in syrup, often enjoyed as a sweet treat. b. Baklava: Layers of filo pastry filled with ground nuts and sweetened with honey or syrup, creating a rich and indulgent dessert. c. Kadaif: A sweet pastry made from shredded dough soaked in syrup and often filled with nuts or cream. d. Štrudla: Macedonian-style apple strudel, with layers of thin pastry filled with cinnamon-spiced apples and nuts.

Macedonian Wines: Macedonia's wine-growing regions, such as Tikves and Povardarie, produce a wide range of quality wines. Macedonian wines are gaining recognition for their unique flavors and grape varieties. Some notable Macedonian wines to try include: a. Vranec: A rich and robust red wine known for its deep red color and fruity flavors, often compared to a bold red from the Mediterranean region. b. Kratoshija: Another red wine variety, known for its smoothness, medium body, and notes of red fruits and spices. c. Žilavka: A white wine made from the indigenous Žilavka grape, offering a crisp and refreshing taste with citrus and floral notes. d. Temjanika: A fragrant white wine with aromas of flowers and stone fruits, often enjoyed as a dessert wine.

Wine Tasting Experiences: Visit local wineries and vineyards to indulge in Macedonian wine tasting experiences. Many wineries offer guided tours where you can learn about the winemaking process, explore the vineyards, and sample a variety of wines. The scenic surroundings and warm hospitality make these wine tasting experiences even more enjoyable.

Chapter 8

Outdoor Adventures

Hiking and Trekking

Macedonia is a hiker's paradise, offering breathtaking landscapes, diverse terrain, and a multitude of hiking and trekking trails for outdoor enthusiasts. Whether you're a seasoned hiker or a beginner looking for a scenic adventure, Macedonia has plenty to offer. Here are some remarkable hiking and trekking destinations in Macedonia:

Mavrovo National Park: Located in the western part of the country, Mavrovo National Park is a stunning mountainous region with diverse trails suitable for all levels of hikers. Explore the pristine forests, sparkling lakes, and majestic peaks as you hike through the park. The highlight is Mount Korab, the highest peak in Macedonia, which offers a challenging trek and rewards you with panoramic views.

Pelister National Park: Nestled in the southwestern part of Macedonia, Pelister National Park is known for its rugged beauty and alpine landscapes. The park is home to Mount Pelister, a popular hiking destination with various trails catering to different fitness levels. As you hike through the park, you'll encounter enchanting forests, glacial lakes, and stunning vistas.

Galichica National Park: Situated between Lake Ohrid and Lake Prespa, Galichica National Park provides an excellent setting for hiking and exploring the natural beauty of the region. The park offers a range of trails that traverse through lush forests, alpine meadows, and picturesque viewpoints, allowing you to soak in the breathtaking views of the surrounding lakes and mountains.

Matka Canyon: Located near the capital city of Skopje, Matka Canyon is a popular destination for outdoor enthusiasts. The canyon offers a variety of hiking trails that lead you through stunning landscapes, towering cliffs, and along the turquoise waters of the Treska River. Don't miss the opportunity to visit the Vrelo Cave, one of the deepest underwater caves in the world.

Shar Mountain: The Shar Mountain range, stretching across the border between Macedonia and Kosovo, is a haven for hikers seeking pristine nature and breathtaking views. The trails in this region vary in difficulty, offering options for both experienced trekkers and beginners. Enjoy the rugged beauty of the mountains, encounter rich flora and fauna, and experience the tranquility of the remote landscapes.

Galichica National Park: Located in the southwestern part of Macedonia, Galichica National Park is a haven for outdoor enthusiasts. The park is renowned for its diverse hiking trails that wind through lush forests, alpine meadows, and offer stunning panoramic views of Lake Ohrid and Lake Prespa. Hike to the peak of Mount Galichica for a truly awe-inspiring experience.

Jablanica Mountain: Situated in the eastern part of Macedonia, Jablanica Mountain is an excellent destination for hikers looking for unspoiled wilderness and challenging trails. The mountain offers a range of routes that lead you through dense forests, rugged terrains, and alpine meadows. Explore the untouched beauty of this region and be rewarded with breathtaking vistas.

Rock Climbing and Mountaineering

Macedonia offers a fantastic playground for rock climbers and mountaineers, with its diverse mountainous terrain and stunning rock formations. Whether you're a seasoned climber or a beginner looking to try your hand at this thrilling sport, Macedonia has a range of options to satisfy your adventurous spirit. Here are some notable rock climbing and mountaineering destinations in Macedonia:

Matka Canyon: Matka Canyon, located near Skopje, not only offers hiking opportunities but is also a popular spot for rock climbing. The vertical limestone cliffs that line the canyon provide excellent routes for climbers of all levels. With various climbing routes and stunning views of the canyon and the Treska River, Matka Canyon is a must-visit destination for rock climbing enthusiasts.

Shar Mountain: Shar Mountain, situated on the border between Macedonia and Kosovo, is a paradise for mountaineers. With its towering peaks and challenging terrains, it offers thrilling opportunities for advanced mountaineering expeditions. Mount Titov Vrv, the highest peak in Shar Mountain, provides a formidable challenge for experienced climbers seeking a thrilling ascent.

Baba Mountain: Baba Mountain, located in the southwestern part of Macedonia, offers a range of mountaineering opportunities. The diverse terrain of Baba Mountain includes rocky peaks, deep valleys, and alpine meadows. Climbers can explore various routes that cater to different skill levels, with stunning views of the surrounding landscapes as their reward.

Kratovo Bouldering: The town of Kratovo, known for its historic charm, is also a hidden gem for bouldering enthusiasts. The unique rock formations and cliffs in and around Kratovo provide excellent bouldering opportunities. Climbers can test their skills and problem-solving abilities on the challenging boulders, surrounded by the town's picturesque surroundings.

Plakenska Mountain: Plakenska Mountain, located in the Pelagonia region, is a lesser-known but promising destination for rock climbing. With its rugged limestone cliffs and challenging routes, it offers a thrilling experience for climbers seeking adventure off the beaten path. The stunning landscapes and panoramic views from the summits make it a worthwhile destination for mountaineers.

Demir Kapija Gorge: Situated in the south of Macedonia, the Demir Kapija Gorge is not only famous for its stunning natural beauty but also offers rock climbing opportunities. The steep limestone cliffs and vertical walls of the gorge provide a challenging playground for climbers. From beginner-friendly routes to more advanced challenges, climbers of all levels can find something to suit their abilities.

When engaging in rock climbing and mountaineering activities in Macedonia, it's crucial to prioritize safety and be equipped with the necessary gear, including helmets, harnesses, and appropriate climbing shoes. It is also advisable to climb with experienced local guides who are familiar with the routes and can ensure a safe and enjoyable experience.

Skiing and Winter Sports

Macedonia may not be the first destination that comes to mind when thinking of skiing and winter sports, but it offers fantastic opportunities for winter enthusiasts. With its mountainous terrain and snowy winters, Macedonia provides a unique winter sports experience. Here are some of the top skiing and winter sports destinations in the country:

Mavrovo Ski Resort: Located in the Mavrovo National Park, the Mavrovo Ski Resort is the largest and most popular ski resort in Macedonia. It offers a range of ski slopes catering to all levels of skiers, from beginners to advanced. With modern facilities, ski schools, and equipment rentals, Mavrovo Ski Resort provides everything you need for an enjoyable skiing experience.

Popova Shapka Ski Resort: Situated in the Shar Mountain range, Popova Shapka Ski Resort is known for its challenging slopes and stunning alpine scenery. It is a favorite destination among experienced skiers and snowboarders. The resort offers a variety of runs, including off-piste options, as well as facilities such as ski lifts, equipment rentals, and cozy mountain lodges.

Kozuf Ski Resort: Located in the southern part of Macedonia, near the town of Gevgelija, Kozuf Ski Resort offers a unique skiing experience. Nestled in the Kozuf Mountain range, this resort provides breathtaking views and well-groomed slopes suitable for all skill levels. It is an ideal destination for families and beginners looking to learn and enjoy winter sports.

Pelister National Park: Pelister National Park, in addition to its hiking trails, transforms into a winter wonderland during the colder months. The park's peaks, including Mount Pelister, offer opportunities for ski touring and backcountry skiing. Experienced skiers can explore the pristine snowy landscapes and enjoy the thrill of untouched powder snow.

Krusevo: Known as the highest town in Macedonia, Krusevo becomes a hub for winter sports enthusiasts during the winter season. It offers a combination of ski slopes, snowboarding parks, and cross-country skiing trails. Krusevo is an excellent destination for those seeking a winter sports adventure in a charming and picturesque setting.

Snowshoeing and Winter Hiking: For those who prefer a slower pace, snowshoeing and winter hiking are popular activities in Macedonia. Explore the snowy landscapes, forests, and mountain trails at your own pace, immersing yourself in the tranquility of the winter scenery. Places like Mavrovo National Park and Pelister National Park provide excellent opportunities for snowshoeing and winter hiking.

River Rafting and Kayaking

Macedonia might not be the first destination that comes to mind for river rafting and kayaking, but the country offers thrilling opportunities for water sports enthusiasts. With its pristine rivers, dramatic canyons, and stunning landscapes, Macedonia provides an exciting playground for river rafting and kayaking adventures. Here are some of the top spots for river rafting and kayaking in the country:

Treska River: The Treska River, located near Skopje, offers excellent opportunities for river rafting and kayaking. With its clear turquoise waters and exciting rapids, it provides an adrenaline-pumping experience for water sports enthusiasts. The Treska Canyon, with its towering cliffs and picturesque surroundings, adds to the thrill of the adventure.

Vardar River: The Vardar River, the longest river in Macedonia, is another great destination for river rafting and kayaking. The river flows through diverse landscapes, including gorges, valleys, and plains, offering a variety of experiences for water sports enthusiasts. From calm sections perfect for kayaking to exhilarating rapids for rafting, the Vardar River has something for everyone.

Radika River: The Radika River, located in the western part of Macedonia, is known for its scenic beauty and challenging rapids. It offers an exciting and adventurous experience for experienced rafters and kayakers. Surrounded by breathtaking landscapes and deep canyons, the Radika River promises an unforgettable journey through its wild waters.

Crna River: The Crna River, located near the town of Struga, is a hidden gem for river rafting and kayaking. This river flows through a picturesque valley and offers a combination of tranquil sections and thrilling rapids. As you navigate the

Crna River's twists and turns, you'll be surrounded by lush greenery and stunning natural scenery.

Bregalnica River: The Bregalnica River, in the eastern part of Macedonia, is a fantastic destination for kayaking enthusiasts. With its calm waters and beautiful landscapes, it provides a peaceful and serene kayaking experience. Explore the river's meandering flow, pass by charming villages, and enjoy the tranquility of the surrounding nature.

When participating in river rafting and kayaking activities in Macedonia, it is essential to prioritize safety and follow the guidance of experienced guides. It is advisable to wear appropriate safety gear and have basic knowledge of paddling techniques. Many local adventure companies offer guided tours and equipment rental services, ensuring a safe and enjoyable experience on the water.

Wildlife and Nature Reserves

Macedonia is home to a rich diversity of wildlife and boasts several nature reserves and protected areas that offer a glimpse into the country's natural wonders. From majestic mountains to tranquil lakes, these habitats provide a sanctuary for various plant and animal species. Here are some notable wildlife and nature reserves in Macedonia:

Galicica National Park: Situated between Lake Ohrid and Lake Prespa, Galicica National Park is a pristine wilderness that encompasses the Galicica Mountain range. The park is known for its diverse flora and fauna, including rare orchids and endemic species. Visitors can explore the park's hiking trails, enjoy panoramic views, and spot wildlife such as chamois, bears, wolves, and a variety of bird species.

Pelister National Park: Located in the Baba Mountain range, Pelister National Park is one of the oldest and most renowned national parks in Macedonia. The park's diverse landscapes range from alpine meadows to dense forests and glacial lakes. It is home to rare plant species, such as the Macedonian pine, and wildlife including Balkan chamois, bears, wolves, and numerous bird species.

Mavrovo National Park: Mavrovo National Park, the largest national park in Macedonia, is a nature lover's paradise. Nestled in the western part of the country, it features impressive mountain ranges, deep canyons, and the beautiful Mavrovo Lake. The park is inhabited by diverse wildlife, including bears, lynx, wolves, chamois, and various bird species. Visitors can enjoy hiking, wildlife watching, and winter sports in this stunning natural setting.

Lake Ohrid: Lake Ohrid, a UNESCO World Heritage site, is not only known for its cultural and historical significance but also for its ecological importance. The lake is home to unique species of fish, including the Ohrid trout, as well as various migratory bird species. Exploring the lake by boat allows visitors to appreciate its natural beauty and encounter its rich biodiversity.

Lake Prespa: Shared between Macedonia, Albania, and Greece, Lake Prespa is another important natural treasure. It is one of Europe's oldest lakes and provides a vital habitat for numerous bird species, including the Dalmatian pelican, cormorants, and herons. Birdwatchers and nature enthusiasts can explore the lake's surroundings, observe the avian residents, and appreciate the peaceful ambiance.

Dojran Lake: Located in the southeastern part of Macedonia, Dojran Lake is a small but significant freshwater lake. It is renowned for its therapeutic properties due to its high salt content. The lake and its surrounding wetlands are home to various bird species, including flamingos, making it an important stop for birdwatchers.

Chapter 9

Practical Tips for Travelers

Local Etiquette and Customs

When visiting Macedonia, it's essential to familiarize yourself with the local etiquette and customs to ensure a respectful and pleasant experience. Here are some key aspects of Macedonian etiquette:

Greetings and Politeness: Macedonians generally greet each other with a handshake and direct eye contact. It is customary to address people by their first name followed by their patronymic (father's name) as a sign of respect. Use "Gospodin" for Mr. and "Gospodja" for Mrs. or Miss, followed by the person's surname. Politeness and courtesy are highly valued in Macedonian culture.

Dress Code: Macedonians tend to dress modestly, particularly in more formal or religious settings. When visiting churches or monasteries, it is advisable to dress conservatively, covering your shoulders and knees. In everyday situations, casual attire is generally acceptable.

Punctuality and Respect for Time: Macedonians appreciate punctuality and expect others to be on time for appointments and social gatherings. It is considered polite to notify the host if you anticipate being late. Being respectful of people's time is highly valued in Macedonian culture.

Dining Etiquette: When invited to someone's home for a meal, it is customary to bring a small gift such as flowers or chocolates for the host. Macedonian cuisine is typically served family-style, with shared dishes. It is polite to try a bit of everything and to compliment the cook. Avoid discussing sensitive topics during meals and refrain from leaving food on your plate as it may be seen as wasteful.

Hospitality and Generosity: Macedonians are known for their warm hospitality. When invited into someone's home, it is customary to remove your shoes at the entrance unless instructed otherwise. Guests are often offered refreshments and treated with generosity. It is polite to express gratitude and thank your hosts for their hospitality.

Cultural Sensitivity: Respect for Macedonia's diverse cultural heritage is important. Be mindful of religious sites and customs, dress appropriately, and behave respectfully when visiting them. Avoid discussing sensitive political or historical topics unless initiated by your local hosts. Taking photographs of people without permission is considered impolite, so always ask for consent.

Tipping: Tipping is customary in Macedonia. In restaurants, it is customary to leave a tip of around 10% of the bill. Taxi drivers can be tipped by rounding up the fare. While tipping is appreciated, it is not mandatory, and the decision to tip should be based on the quality of service received.

Health and Safety Precautions

North Macedonia is a generally safe country to travel to, but there are a few health and safety precautions that first-time visitors should take.

Vaccinations

The Centers for Disease Control and Prevention (CDC) recommends that all travelers to North Macedonia be up-to-date on their routine vaccinations, including measles, mumps, rubella, polio, tetanus, diphtheria, and pertussis. In addition, the CDC recommends that travelers to North Macedonia get vaccinated against hepatitis A and B, as well as typhoid.

Travel Insurance

It is also important to purchase travel insurance before traveling to North Macedonia. This will protect you in case you need medical care while you are there. Travel insurance should also cover medical evacuation, in case you need to be flown home for treatment.

Water and Food

The tap water in North Macedonia is not safe to drink. Only bottled water or water that has been boiled should be consumed. You should also be careful about the food you eat. Avoid street food, and make sure that any food you eat is cooked thoroughly.

Sun and Heat

North Macedonia can get very hot in the summer, so it is important to protect yourself from the sun. Wear sunscreen with an SPF of 30 or higher, and a hat and sunglasses. Drink plenty of fluids, and avoid being outside during the hottest part of the day.

Crime

Petty theft is the most common crime in North Macedonia. To avoid being a victim of theft, be aware of your surroundings at all times, and do not leave your belongings unattended. You should also be careful when using ATMs, as there have been reports of skimming.

Political Situation

North Macedonia is a relatively stable country, but there have been some recent political protests. If you are planning to travel to North Macedonia during a time of political unrest, it is important to be aware of the situation and take precautions to stay safe.

Other Precautions

Here are some other health and safety precautions to take when traveling to North Macedonia:

Be aware of the risks of altitude sickness if you are planning to visit the mountains.

If you are traveling with children, make sure they are up-to-date on their vaccinations and that they have a medical kit with them.

If you have any chronic health conditions, make sure you have a doctor's letter with you stating your condition and what medications you take.

By following these health and safety precautions, you can help to ensure a safe and enjoyable trip to North Macedonia.

Communication and Internet Access

Communication and internet access in Macedonia are generally reliable and convenient for travelers. Here's what you need to know about staying connected during your visit:

Mobile Network Coverage: Macedonia has well-developed mobile network coverage, offering reliable voice and data services throughout the country. The major mobile network operators in Macedonia include Makedonski Telekom, A1 Macedonia, and VIP Operator. Make sure your mobile phone is unlocked or compatible with international SIM cards to use local services.

SIM Cards and Prepaid Plans: To have a local number and enjoy affordable rates for calls, text messages, and data, you can purchase a prepaid SIM card from one of the mobile network providers. SIM cards are readily available at airports, mobile operator stores, and various retail outlets. For registration, you must have your passport on hand. Consider choosing a plan that suits your needs, whether it's for local calls, international calls, or data usage.

Wi-Fi Availability: Wi-Fi access is widely available in Macedonia, especially in hotels, cafes, restaurants, and public spaces. Many accommodations offer complimentary Wi-Fi for guests, and numerous cafes and restaurants provide free Wi-Fi as well. It's always a good idea to check with your accommodation for the availability and details of their Wi-Fi service.

Internet Cafes: While internet cafes are not as prevalent as they once were, you can still find them in major cities and tourist areas. Internet cafes typically offer computers with internet access for a fee, allowing you to surf the web, check emails, or make video calls if you don't have your own device.

Roaming: If you prefer to use your existing mobile number and plan, check with your home mobile network provider about international roaming options in Macedonia. Be aware that roaming charges can be high, so it's advisable to carefully review the rates and data allowances before using this option.

Messaging and Voice over Internet Protocol (VoIP) Apps: To save on international calling and messaging costs, consider using messaging apps or VoIP services that rely on internet connectivity. Popular options include WhatsApp, Viber, Skype, and Facebook Messenger. These apps allow you to make voice and video calls, send messages, and share media files using Wi-Fi or mobile data.

Recommended Travel Apps

To enhance your travel experience in Macedonia, here are some recommended travel apps that can assist you with navigation, language translation, currency conversion, and local recommendations:

Maps.me: Maps.me is a reliable offline mapping app that provides detailed maps and navigation without the need for an internet connection. You can download maps of Macedonia in advance and use them to navigate cities, find attractions, and locate accommodations, even when you're offline.

Google Maps: Google Maps is a versatile navigation app that offers detailed maps, real-time traffic updates, and public transportation information. It can be used online or offline, and it provides directions, reviews, and recommendations for restaurants, attractions, and other points of interest.

XE Currency: XE Currency is a trusted app for currency conversion, allowing you to quickly calculate exchange rates between different currencies. It updates the rates regularly and provides a user-friendly interface for easy conversion on-the-go.

Google Translate: Google Translate is an invaluable app for overcoming language barriers. It offers translations between various languages, including Macedonian, and provides options for typing, speaking, or even using the camera to translate text in real-time. It can be a helpful tool for communicating with locals and understanding signs and menus.

Tripadvisor: Tripadvisor is a popular travel app that provides reviews, ratings, and recommendations for hotels, restaurants, attractions, and activities. It can help you find top-rated establishments in Macedonia, read traveler reviews, and make informed decisions about where to visit and dine.

Booking.com or Airbnb: These apps are useful for finding and booking accommodations in Macedonia. Booking.com offers a wide range of hotels, hostels, and guesthouses, while Airbnb provides options for unique and local stays. Both apps allow you to filter by location, price range, and amenities, making it easy to find suitable accommodations for your preferences.

Visit Macedonia: The Visit Macedonia app is an official tourism app that offers comprehensive information about attractions, events, accommodations, and transportation in the country. It provides detailed descriptions, photos, and maps to help you plan your itinerary and discover the best of Macedonia.

Useful Phrases in Macedonian

Learning a few basic phrases in the local language can greatly enhance your travel experience in Macedonia and show your appreciation for the culture. Here are some useful phrases in Macedonian:

Hello - Здраво (Zdravo)

Goodbye - Довидување (Doviduvanje)

Thank you - Ви благодарам (Vi blagodaram)

Please - Ве молам (Ve molam)

Yes - Да (Da)

No - Не (Ne)

Excuse me - Извинете (Izvinete)

Sorry - Се извинувам (Se izvinuvam)

Do you speak English? - Зборувате ли англиски? (Zboruvate li angliski?)

I don't understand - Не разбирам (Ne razbiram)

How much does it cost? - Колку чини? (Kolku chini?)

Where is the bathroom? - Каде е тоалетот? (Kade e toaletot?)

I would like... - Сакам... (Sakam...)

Can you help me? - Можете ли да ми помогнете? (Mozhete li da mi pomognete?)

Cheers! (Toasting) - Наздравје! (Nazdravje!)

Remember, making an effort to speak a few words in Macedonian is appreciated by locals and can help you connect with them on a more personal level. Don't be afraid to practice these phrases and embrace the local language during your visit to Macedonia.

Conclusion and Additional Resources

Recap of Must-See Places and Experiences

To recap, here are the must-see places and experiences in Macedonia that you should include in your itinerary:

Skopje City:

Explore the Skopje Fortress and enjoy panoramic views of the city.

Visit the Old Bazaar, one of the largest and oldest bazaars in the Balkans.

Discover the unique architectural styles at the Macedonian Square and the Triumphal Arch.

Marvel at the stunning Macedonian Orthodox Cathedral of Saint Clement of Ohrid.

Take a leisurely stroll along the Stone Bridge, a symbol of Skopje.

Ohrid City and Lake:

Explore the picturesque Old Town of Ohrid, a UNESCO World Heritage site.

Visit the iconic Ohrid Lake, known for its crystal-clear waters and stunning landscapes.

Discover the historic Samuil's Fortress and enjoy panoramic views of the lake.

Explore the ancient Plaoshnik Archaeological Site and the Church of St. John at Kaneo.

Take a boat ride on the lake and visit the charming St. Naum Monastery.

Matka Canyon:

Embark on a boat tour through the breathtaking Matka Canyon.

Visit the Vrelo Cave, known for its stunning stalactite formations.

Enjoy hiking and nature walks in the surrounding area, discovering hidden monasteries and waterfalls.

Mavrovo National Park:

Experience the beauty of Mavrovo National Park, known for its pristine lakes and mountain landscapes.

Enjoy skiing, snowboarding, and other winter sports during the snowy season.

Explore hiking trails and discover the charming village of Mavrovo.

Bitola and Pelister National Park:

Visit Bitola, a city rich in history and architectural heritage.

Explore the ancient ruins of Heraclea Lyncestis, an important archaeological site.

Discover the natural wonders of Pelister National Park and hike to the peak of Mount Pelister for breathtaking views.

Kratovo and Kuklica Stone Dolls:

Explore the charming town of Kratovo, known for its medieval architecture and stone bridges.

Visit the unique Kuklica Stone Dolls, a natural phenomenon featuring bizarre rock formations.

Stobi Archaeological Site:

Discover the ancient ruins of Stobi, an important archaeological site showcasing Roman and Byzantine history.

Explore the well-preserved amphitheater, basilicas, and mosaics.

Macedonian Festivals and Events:

Experience the vibrant Macedonian culture by attending traditional festivals, such as the Ohrid Summer Festival, Skopje Jazz Festival, or the Strumica Carnival.

Macedonian Cuisine and Wine Tasting:

Indulge in the delicious Macedonian cuisine, featuring dishes like Tavče Gravče (bean stew) and Ajvar (red pepper relish).

Visit local wineries and enjoy wine tastings, as Macedonia is known for its excellent wine production.

Outdoor Adventures:

Engage in outdoor activities like hiking, trekking, and rock climbing in the country's stunning natural landscapes.

Enjoy water sports such as river rafting and kayaking in Macedonia's rivers.

These are just a few highlights of what Macedonia has to offer. Each destination and experience will provide unique insights into the country's rich history, natural beauty, and warm hospitality. Make sure to plan your itinerary accordingly and create lasting memories in this remarkable Balkan gem.